Financial Nutrition® for Young Women

Financial Nutrition®
for Young Women

How (and Why) to Teach Girls about Money

Melissa Donohue, EdD

Foreword by Molly Donohue

PRAEGER™

An Imprint of ABC-CLIO, LLC

Santa Barbara, California • Denver, Colorado

Library of Congress Cataloging-in-Publication Data

Names: Donohue, Melissa, author.
Title: Financial nutrition for young women : how (and why) to teach girls about money / Melissa Donohue, EdD.
Description: Santa Barbara, California : Praeger, [2017] | Includes bibliographical references and index.
Identifiers: LCCN 2017025129 (print) | LCCN 2017036294 (ebook) |
    ISBN 9781440852312 (ebook) | ISBN 9781440852305 (hardcopy : alk. paper)
Subjects: LCSH: Financial literacy. | Young women—Finance, Personal. |
    Finance, Personal.
Classification: LCC HG179 (ebook) | LCC HG179 .D633 2018 (print) |
    DDC 332.0240084/22—dc23
LC record available at https://lccn.loc.gov/2017025129

ISBN: 978-1-4408-5230-5
EISBN: 978-1-4408-5231-2

21 20 19 18 17   1 2 3 4 5

This book is also available as an eBook.

Praeger
An Imprint of ABC-CLIO, LLC

ABC-CLIO, LLC
130 Cremona Drive, P.O. Box 1911
Santa Barbara, California 93116-1911
www.abc-clio.com

This book is printed on acid-free paper ∞

Manufactured in the United States of America

*To my daughter and all young women in their quest for
financial independence and economic empowerment*

Contents

Foreword

Molly Donohue

When I was 15 years old, an age when most of us are incredibly aware of what others think of us, my mother Melissa Donohue began teaching an optional class at my high school. Initially, I was filled with dread at the prospect of my mother working at my school. What would people think? I soon learned that I never should have doubted my mother's talent or charisma. One day as I was walking through the halls of the mansion that was my Upper East Side all-girls school, I overheard a group of girls engaged in a lively conversation about women's finance—topics they had learned in my mother's class. I instantly recognized the conversation as it was similar to debates that had filled the walls of my home from the time I was small. I also have distinct memories of the girls in my mother's class raising relevant points they had learned about finance from her class, in the history and English classes I was a part of. Later in the year, when I participated in the "obligatory" Mother's Day Instagram post, one of my mother's students, who was also a friend of mine, commented, "I like your mom as much as you!"

In addition to the fact that my mother, at the age of 46, was seemingly able to become popular among a group of teenaged girls, I learned that my mother has a very unique talent for teaching and inspiring young women. Not only did those girls learn about basic financial concepts, but my mother was able to inspire a deep interest and excitement in many of them, a sign of a very unique and very talented teacher.

The interest and excitement that she inspired in those young women in only five classes are absolutely essential in a world where women still make 78 cents to the dollar and are still ending their lives with less money than their male counterparts. *Financial Nutrition® for Young Women: How (and Why) to Teach Girls about Money* presents topics for parents that are fundamental to 21st-century feminism. This book does not beg young women to abandon motherhood or go into STEM-related fields that will pay them greater salaries, but simply presents the necessary information to make choices that will lead them to a happier and more financially stable life.

And as my mother's favorite student/guinea pig, I can say with confidence that this method works. Having had these conversations with the author and participated in many of these exercises, I feel prepared to have a successful financial future. I know I will be able to ask for a raise with grace and confidence when I know I am deserving and to invest wisely. I hope this book leads you and your daughter to the meaningful discussions about money that I was so fortunate to grow up with.

Preface

I was pissed.

I had been toiling away for months on my doctoral dissertation, which focused on how to address issues around women's financial literacy. I based my work on the generally accepted premise that women were not particularly financially literate. But the more I researched, the more I realized that women's perceived lack of "financial literacy" was related more to their diminished access to capital and their life priorities than to their understanding of how money works. In fact, I found that women's financial literacy was well beyond what the current literature suggested. Perhaps it should have come as no surprise that the popularly accepted analysis of women's financial literacy was flawed, given my own career path. I had worked successfully in finance, financial journalism, and financial education, and I was, indeed, a woman.

Although doctoral research is all about contributing new knowledge to the field, I did not imagine I'd discover something quite so groundbreaking. And it rocked my world. It rocked my world so hard that my research discoveries eventually became the basis for and the underlying philosophy of my Financial Nutrition® organization and this book. But first, more about my story.

I knew I needed to finish graduate school in a reasonable amount of time so I could return to a semblance of a "normal" life with one full-time job instead of three part-time ones, more than a few hours of sleep a night, and consistent cash flow so that I could not just pay my mortgage each month but also have some discretionary income. Despite some skepticism that I would discover anything genuinely new, I was excited to conduct research into women's financial literacy. I loved my topic. It somehow managed to make my entire life make sense, including my feminist upbringing, what felt like a patchwork quilt of a resume, and my seemingly incompatible strengths as a high school educator on one hand and a financial analyst on the other. The study of women's financial literacy brought my life together into one strong, cohesive, logical thread, and as I researched, I realized financial literacy could well have that impact on other women.

I understood finance and economics, and believed in women's equality and empowerment in all areas. I also believed in financial education and had experienced its efficacy as a teacher and a student. But another key factor in my interest in women's financial literacy was that I was an anomaly. In graduate school I found that I was considered unique as a financially literate woman. I probably should not have been surprised: studies show over and over again that women are a less financially literate group, along with African Americans, Hispanics, and other oppressed groups in the United States.

I focused my doctoral research on the types of education women needed most in order to become financially literate. Money is a huge area—it's social, emotional, quantitative, and many other things—and I wanted to make sure to define my research so that I could do a cogent study. Since my degree would be in education, I attacked the huge women's financial literacy puzzle with an educational focus. Some of what I found did not come as a surprise. Surveys I reviewed showed that women were well versed in the "home economic" areas, like budgeting, but knew less about more complex financial areas, like investing and mortgages. The behavioral research showed that although women were the fastest growing group of mortgage holders, they had far less invested for retirement, and had a much larger percentage of subprime mortgages during the mortgage crisis, and a subsequent higher number of mortgage defaults.[1]

Some of what I found *was* a surprise. Interestingly, women were given a higher number of subprime mortgages even when they had the same credit scores as men. That one stayed with me—a subprime mortgage is typically based on the riskiness of the borrower, which is determined in part by the borrower's credit score. So what was happening with women that they were getting crappier mortgages than they deserved?[2]

Finally, I had conversations with actual women. My focus groups were lower-income women who were participating in a financial literacy class. And what I found was that these women understood—and were utilizing and implementing—fairly sophisticated economic concepts, well beyond what they were learning in the class. They thought in terms of value, risk, and opportunity costs. They understood the concept of investing as a way of using money to make more money. They knew they should be saving for retirement. In fact, these women were living, eating, and breathing complex financial concepts and decisions on a daily basis.[3]

But what was missing for these women? If they had the knowledge, why weren't they behaving in what I had defined as a "financially literate" way? Why weren't they reaping the benefits of that literacy: living in style, sending their kids to private schools, owning second (or any) homes, going on vacation like the financial guys I had worked with in New York?

Then it hit me, and as I said before, I was pissed.

I had made a lot of assumptions in my efforts to understand the barriers surrounding women's financial literacy. I accepted the premise that financial knowledge leads to responsible financial behavior, that the marriage of knowledge and behavior in the financial realm was happy and automatic. I accepted a foundational concept of economics, that humans are motivated by their self-interest and "utility maximization" (in other words, to maximize the total value derived from money) and behave "rationally" in that pursuit. But as it turns out my assumptions clouded a dramatic truth—that the concept of financial literacy was deeply flawed with respect to women.

My first realization was that access to capital, or having money, has a huge impact on a person's ability to be financially responsible. If you're underpaid, underemployed, or do not have the capital to invest and grow wealth, it's going to be damn near impossible to save for retirement, invest and build wealth, obtain a high-quality mortgage, and pay off credit cards. In other words, even if you have the financial knowledge about what you should be doing, you do not have the capital to put that knowledge into practice.

My second realization came around the issue of priorities. Sure, economics is based on the concept of a "rational actor" who "maximizes utility" financially. But guess what—not all people have the same idea of what's "rational" or of the meaning of "utility." Because these women's priorities involved using their limited capital to take care of their kids and not saving for their own retirement, they were not maximizing their utility. They were deemed "irrational" from an economic sense and financially irresponsible. Looking at the original financial literacy logic, that irresponsible financial behavior indicates that they are not financially literate.

A parallel can be drawn between economics and medical research, where the vast majority of clinical studies undertaken have been conducted on men. The singular perspective tends to lead to conclusions that are either wrong or reveal only part of the story. Medicine is slowly addressing this bias, and a similar reevaluation needs to happen in finance. My research showed me that just as women's wellness and pathology cannot be judged according to a preordained, "male" standard, women's financial literacy could not be understood in terms of the traditional definitions of the concept, so I expanded my definition of financial literacy to include access to capital, as an aspect of the behavioral component. In other words, financial literacy on its own did not equal responsible financial behavior, and by the same token, financial behavior that does not appear to be responsible, or rational, indicates a lack of financial understanding. Having the capital, or money, to put to use is a critical component of financial behavior.

My findings did show me that although women had a core understanding of financial concepts, they needed more education in the areas of investing and mortgages. Intuitive as it may seem, this was powerful information; after all, both of those tools are the primary ways that "normal" consumers can build wealth in the United States. With my later work with women's financial literacy, I learned that women earned less than men and consequently saved less than men. From there it became clear that, given women's limited access to capital and the fact that few women maximize their salary potential, they needed as much information about income sources as they could get.

Despite all of the regulatory changes like the Lilly Ledbetter Fair Pay Act and other class-action suits that have sought to redress economic disparities, women do not head to work on a level playing field. We are still paid 78 cents on the dollar compared to our male counterparts[4] and hold far fewer leadership positions.[5] Women are more likely to bear—sometimes by choice, sometimes out of necessity—the primary responsibility for child care and elder care, which means they may be in and out of the workforce, slowing the momentum of their careers, taking positions and projects that are "off the radar," earning less over a lifetime, which means saving less over a lifetime and being poorer in retirement.[6] All of these issues seem to contribute to women's proven aversion to financial risk, which discourages many women from investing. It seemed to me that women were not as likely to want to put their capital at risk because they had less of it, and it was harder for them to come by.

So in the end, my discoveries about women's financial literacy did not yield a dogma about the types of lives women should choose—whether they should work, or pursue certain careers, or get married, or have kids. My research conclusion was that women need financial knowledge, a behavioral disposition, and access to capital so they can live the lives they choose on their own terms.[7] However, I wanted to teach girls about money because I saw that the key to solving the women's economic power gap could very well be teaching girls and young women how to become financially independent and economically empowered.

Just like other behaviors that are key to women's physical well-being, like annual physicals, maintaining reproductive health, getting regular exercise, and understanding good diet and nutrition, effective financial learning needs to start at a young age in order for it to become habit, to become part of our DNA. We teach kids about nutrition and other kinds of physical self-care so they can grow up into independently healthy adults. In order to help girls become independently financially healthy, we also need to teach them how to take care of themselves with money. Of course I believe that boys also benefit from a financial education, *but it is absolutely critical for girls*, given the desperate economic inequality women face throughout life, and the increasing financial responsibility they are assuming. Teaching young women healthy money behaviors at a young age gives them a better chance to solve life's problems—and seize life's opportunities.

I knew from working with teens in the finance and economic education center I founded in western Massachusetts that young people are extremely capable of taking in and using knowledge about money, and that they were, for the most part, really interested in and concerned about their financial futures. I also know the ugly statistics about gender wage gaps that begin directly after college; that the highest-paying majors, typically in the STEM fields, are still dominated by men;[8] and about girls' insecurity around math and science, and ultimately finance, engineering, and technology. And from my financial background I got the power of compound interest—and the importance of saving early and often. I got the relevance of investment as a wealth builder that needs time to ride out market cycles and the critical piece that earned income plays in the wealth-building equation. Getting this knowledge and learning these behaviors early in life was critical for women as the decisions they made, and the money they saved and invested early on in their lives, could have significant impact on their future well-being.

And there were more reasons for starting the financial education process early with girls. For one, money behavior tends to be social and emotional—meaning we get and internalize messages surrounding money and worth from our family, society, our identity, and our financial behavior is impacted, and even driven, by those messages. So working with younger women means that they have an opportunity to develop confidence and competence with money as they are absorbing any number of more limiting ideas, such as devaluing their opinions or contributions, or feeling that they should sacrifice and not ask for what they deserve. I appreciate the imperative of working with younger people before they had grown into women who have painted themselves into a financial corner, making financial mistakes, or not taking advantage of financial opportunities, that make them unable to lead the lives they really wanted in terms of work, family, home, and achieving their dreams.

And so from this conviction, and mission, my Financial Nutrition® venture was born. In the organization, we teach girls and young women the basics of money management and entrepreneurial thinking so they can lead lives of independence and success, on their own terms. Entrepreneurship learning, and the resulting development of entrepreneurial thinking, comes into play because it involves thinking outside of the societal confines that may box us in, that tell us we can only be financially comfortable if we take a certain work route, or that we are demanding and unlikeable if we go for what it is that we want. Additionally, we sometimes need to realize our dreams through a more creative, less traveled approach to life.

And while I agree that "leaning in" in work and life is a critical disposition for women, before it's time for them to lean in, we need to teach girls about money, finance, and entrepreneurial thinking. Studies show that for children as young as eight, boys are more confident with money than girls and that parents address financial issues differently with boys than with girls.[9] And this is just the beginning of a financial divide that grows as the two genders age, and that creates huge consequences in the lives of women.

In addition, girls and young women need more depth to their financial understanding. In essence, one size does not fit all when it comes to financial decision making. True literacy goes a level deeper, teaching people the building blocks of finance and economics, so they can apply principles to different times in their lives and a range of financial goals. That's why I wrote this book. *Financial Nutrition® : How (and Why) to Teach Girls about Money* shows how to teach teenaged girls healthy attitudes, knowledge, and behaviors around money so they can live financially successful lives.

Financial education for anyone can be hard to come by. For young people who need it most, there are not many opportunities to build knowledge and confidence around money. To begin with, most American schools do not offer any kind of effective, comprehensive financial education. Many states do not require financial or economic education. The academic day in high school is already very full with required classes and college preparatory–focused curriculum. Finding room in the high school schedule for personal finance classes can be a challenge, to say the least.

It is also not generally common for financial education to be taught at home. Despite parents' best intentions, money understanding is frequently not taught at home because many adults do not feel comfortable managing—or discussing—money. *Financial Nutrition®* provides a solution—it is an accessible, collaborative guide that helps adults learn how to talk to girls about money and provides a platform for fun, engaging, and independent learning for teenaged girls. *Financial Nutrition®* also provides a framework and support for girls to independently and proactively form clubs in high school and college, as well as a curriculum that schools can adopt.

With *Financial Nutrition*®, I take a wholly different approach to teaching girls about money than other teen financial education books. To begin with, I utilize my own original financial literacy research focused on girls and women, as well as build on the research of psychologist Carol Gilligan, economists Nancy Folbre and Claudia Goldin, and behavioral economist Annamaria Lusardi. This research clearly shows that the financial behavioral influences on women are several—social, emotional, legal, and economic. What I have also learned through my research is that women understand finance but have had less time to practice, having only gained independent access to credit in the 1970s.[10] I also discovered that women don't always know how to "play the game" when it comes to things like negotiating a job or securing a mortgage, because they are new to the game and did not write the rules.[11]

This combination of economic concepts and behavioral disposition is the basis of my Financial Nutrition® Method, a pedagogy that aims to empower girls around money, developed from my research and the financial education work I have done with girls. It is powerful, to say the least! The Financial Nutrition® Method addresses knowledge, disposition, and behaviors around money. As such, it provides a unique way to engage girls and help them become confident and knowledgeable with money.

In terms of information, this method looks at things like money having a cost, the quantification of risk, the analysis of value, the understanding of opportunity costs, the importance of information and the role of experts. These concepts underlie skills development that is extremely critical for girls and young women today. Beyond just understanding the "home economics" concepts like saving and budgeting, girls need to master the real wealth builders: income development, investing, and mortgages.

As a financial educator, I also see huge value in teaching girls and young women about entrepreneurship, whether or not they aspire to own their own business. Entrepreneurship is all about creativity and resourcefulness, tenacity and resiliency. Every entrepreneur knows she must learn to embrace failure and to learn to bounce back with an even better idea. Entrepreneurship demands a certain amount of fearlessness and measured risk taking, which can be translated more positively into self-confidence and belief in one's own abilities. Idea generation and opportunity recognition are also key to starting a new venture. Whether the venture is for-profit or a social enterprise, entrepreneurship is all about finding a better way, a new way, or maybe even the only way, to help make life better.

Again, I do not aim to teach young women how to live their lives, what to major in in college, whether to have a family, work, or not work. It is, however, true that certain college majors lead to higher-paying careers and that taking time off to have children can have a real and long-term impact on income potential if not managed effectively. These financial dynamics need to be understood, leveraged, or planned for, and my experience in the classroom is that girls and young women are extremely interested in their financial futures and both want, and need, to know this information.

Teaching girls about money can lead to financial literacy and economic empowerment in knowledge and behavior. Providing a framework for parents, clubs, and schools can mean this learning is easy and accessible. With this collaborative and unique approach to learning and financial understanding, *Financial Nutrition*® can change the financial landscape—and possibility for success and financial security—for the women these girls will become.

Acknowledgments

This book has been a project that has been supported by many, many people who believe as I do in women's financial and economic empowerment—too many to thank in this space. I would like to acknowledge and thank two women who made this book happen and believe deeply in its mission, from the very beginning to the very end. Thank you to Jessica Papin at Dystel, Goderich & Bourret, my incredible agent, and Hilary Claggett at ABC-CLIO, my awesome editor. I would also like to give great acknowledgment and love to two women who went far above and beyond the bonds and commitment of sisterhood in my work, and in my life. To Sarah Howard and Patty Donohue, thank you, thank you, thank you!

CHAPTER ONE

Women and Money: Telling the Story for Girls

Why teach girls about money?

Let me tell a story to set the stage for understanding this critical need and its ramifications. I had dinner recently with a good friend who is not only a successful international journalist but also the very happy mother of two little girls. We only get to see each other once a year or so as she lives in Europe, but our conversations usually go about the same way. We talk about our career struggles and successes as women, and the unique challenges we face in achieving those successes. Now that my friend has daughters, with our career choices and struggles as the backdrop, the new focus of the conversation is: "What can we do for our daughters so their success as women comes easier than it has for us?"

I thought right away to the mission of my Financial Nutrition® organization: "We teach girls and young women the basics of money management and entrepreneurship so they can lead a life of independence and success, on their own terms." Many women have struggled with work-life issues that are challenging in multiple ways. Although financial understanding does not necessarily answer every question, it is an incredible foundation for making educated decisions about one's life, career, and goals for success.

Think about it. If a woman opts to leave the workforce for several years to focus on parenting, but wants to eventually return to work, she needs to understand what her financial options are in planning for both an eventual return to the workforce and for saving for retirement. Similarly, if a woman needs to or wants to work full-time but wishes to pursue other interests as well, it may be worthwhile to explore different career paths, including working for herself to maximize time flexibility, income potential, and doing fulfilling work. These issues are ongoing fodder for conversations about work, lifestyle, and parenting, meaning life in general, and a key ingredient to maximizing the results of the conversation is a solid foundation of financial understanding, and wealth creation.

Money is the key to so many life empowerment issues, and women have historically come out on the short end of this. But recently, vast popular coverage shows that the focus on women's financial inequality has hit a tipping point. Major media outlets like *The New York Times*, *The Wall Street Journal*, *The Huffington Post*, Bloomberg, and even *The New Yorker* run breaking news articles, features, and perspective pieces on the issue frequently. Women's economic power in the United States is becoming bigger and bigger news, front and center for Fortune 500 companies, Hollywood award shows, and presidential candidates. The Pandora's box that Sheryl Sandberg opened with the release of her bestseller *Lean In* continues to explode.

But while women's wages rose steadily through the early decades of the 20th century, the momentum has stagnated over the past 20 years, with women currently earning 78 cents on the dollar compared to men.[1] Women make up almost 50 percent of the U.S. workforce,[2] and 40 percent of households with children have a female primary breadwinner.[3] But women are also said to be one of the financially oppressed and illiterate populations. Women earn less, save less, and have a greater fear of investing than men.[4] Given those facts, and the fact that in the United States wealth creation results primarily from earned income and investing, it is no big surprise that women are almost twice as likely as men to end their lives below the poverty line.[5]

Women's lower incomes and lack of confidence with investing have become very real, and dramatic, empowerment issues. Despite government policy, corporate initiatives, and constant media attention, the gender wage gap and ensuing financial inequality has remained an entrenched issue for women, and this gap impacts their financial independence, success, and livelihood. Although women are playing larger roles managing money for themselves and their families, they are still not always comfortable with investing and working with financial professionals. So what's the answer?

Let's first look at why managing money successfully is so complicated. One of the many challenges with money is that money is about a lot of things, not just a financial skill set. Money can mean a lot of different things to different people: love, care, sacrifice, success, failure, anxiety. Money is not simply a means of exchange, with a cost, and the ability to grow wealth or create financial destitution, although it is all of those things too. Money has cultural and societal messages that may be way more powerful in guiding a person's behavior—especially at a subconscious level—than the financial knowledge they actually have.

Because of these societal messages, the precursor to negative money behaviors may become ingrained in women at a young age. The inability to ask for a raise may have as much to do with the conditioning in girls and women to sacrifice and not "brag," as a lack of understanding of how a salary compounds over time. Girls also learn to be risk-averse and play it safe. They learn to reflect instead of project, not take credit, and keep their opinions hidden if it impacts a relationship. They learn to be supportive and supported, and are rewarded for all of these behaviors as children.[6] Risk aversion comes into play later in life with a lower confidence in investing.[7] Not articulating an opinion can create problems for women when self-advocating with the financial services industry. Failing to speak up, self-promote, acknowledge personal successes, or "brag" can impact a career—and salary potential—in countless negative ways.

And the problems do not just end there. Although women are clearly entering the workforce in greater numbers, gender inequality is still rampant in the workplace, according to a report by the Center for Research on Gender in the Professions at UC San Diego. Women are still underrepresented in the three industries the report examined: law, medicine, and science and technology. Women currently make up only 21 percent of scientists and engineers employed in business and industry. In medicine, women make up only 34 percent of physicians.[8]

Money similarly enters into the picture when you consider things like the highest paid college majors. According to a recent *Wall Street Journal* article, 7 of the top 10 highest paid college majors are engineering-related.[9] It is a well-known fact that fewer women go into STEM-related fields—some estimates show only 23 percent of workers in STEM-related fields are women, while women now make up about half of the overall workforce.[10] Despite some forward motion of women in top tech jobs, the dearth of women in science, engineering, and technology remains an important issue.

These issues may very well be multiple-causative. As we think about raising girls who can be champions to themselves and make their own dreams come true, it is important to think about what we teach our daughters when it comes to money independence, career choice, and following their interests. Not everyone is made to be a scientist or engineer, but giving our daughters the tools they need to discover their potential may well help pave their way to financial independence and personal championship.

So what do our girls need to learn now to manifest their ambition—to succeed in the real world—as they grow to adulthood? How can we send them on their way to be global leaders, captains of industry, and social innovators, if that is who they want to be? How can we empower them economically for any career they choose, or motherhood, or a combination of the two? In other words, how can girls learn to own their power, and become financially independent and successful, even if it seems contrary to everything they learn, and see, in society?

My work experience—and the knowledge and observations I gained from it—can provide the beginning of an explanation. I had an unusual career path, as I was a woman who went into finance. This track was initially a surprise, even to me. After graduating from a small liberal arts college and working in New York City in not-for-profit organizations with an idea of becoming a legal aid attorney, I received full funding through a global leadership program at Columbia University for a master's degree in International Affairs. My career in finance began in a graduate school internship, analyzing Latin American countries' economic policies and political systems at a large European bank. Before long, I discovered that I had an affinity for the incredible story that is the global economic system, with the constant experimentation all governments do to find a way to take care of their people through exchange rate policy, flow of funds, interest rates, and financial support systems.

I got it too. I understood money, finance, and economics in a way that felt natural and organic. This was no small surprise. My parents don't get it. Most of my friends don't get it. I can still remember having dinner with a friend back in the mid-1990s and telling her excitedly about the Latin American debt crisis, sovereign borrowing, and distressed debt restructuring. My friend just stared blankly across the table at me, before finally blurting out, "Seriously, how do you know all this stuff?!"

I was really lucky to work closely with some amazing men who for the lack of a better, less corny shorthand, I would call my "money mentors." These people had finance and economics running through their veins at an even more basic and foundational level than I did. Finance was so natural for these guys that they didn't just *love* it, they *were* it. It was just the way their minds worked—constantly calculating risk and value and opportunity costs in everything they did, from a clothes-buying strategy, to their kids' college education, to the amazing deals they put together on the trading floor. Money didn't cause them anxiety or impact their feelings of self-worth or necessarily define them in any way. Sure, they liked having money, and second homes, and vacations, private schools for their kids, wives who didn't have to work. But at the end of the day, they were really just doing what they knew how to do, and what came naturally to them, and it just so happened it paid fabulously well—not a bad thing, right?

Never once did I believe that because so many of the people I worked with in finance were male, that only men could understand money, or be successful with it. This is despite the fact that I knew the ugly statistics about the gender wage gap that begin directly after college; that the highest-paying majors, typically in the STEM fields, are still dominated by men; and about girls' insecurity around math and science, and ultimately finance, engineering, and technology. Working in finance helped me understand quickly the power of compound interest, which means a dramatic increase in wealth if you start saving early. I very quickly learned and understood the critical value of investing as a wealth builder, but also that investors need lots of time on their sides to ride out the inevitable market cycles— the twists and turns in the market and the economy that can destroy wealth much more quickly than it creates it. I understood how earned income, as well as investment income, was a huge component of the wealth creation puzzle for those of us not lucky enough to be born independently wealthy.

Eventually, I understood that getting this knowledge and learning these behaviors early was an even greater need for women, and that the financial actions they took, and life decisions they made early in their lives could dramatically impact every component of their futures. early on could have significant impact over the course of their lives. I realized too that this information did not portend a dogma about the types of lives women should choose—whether they should work, or pursue certain careers, or get married, or have kids. But I did understand absolutely from my years working in finance that women need financial knowledge, a behavioral disposition, and access to capital so they can live the lives they choose, on their own terms.

I thought for a long time about how to put my findings to work in a context that would make a difference. It seemed to me that there are a good many sources aimed at improving financial literacy among grown women. I wanted to get to girls in this learning area because I saw that the key to solving the women's economic power gap could very well be teaching girls and young women about money so they could make the right decisions early and have the knowledge and disposition to take the right steps throughout their lives.

I know from my doctoral research that although women had a core understanding of financial concepts, they needed more education in the areas of investing and mortgages. I learned, as was my case, that some women either choose to or have to take a less linear career path because of other priorities in their lives like having and raising children. Society, and often family, teach women to care for others and to sacrifice. This disposition is in direct contradiction with the rational-based economic system, where individuals seek to maximize their own personal financial potential as a priority. Our economic system functions this way and is not going to become completely dismantled just because a bunch of women have joined the workforce.

Having learned firsthand what women know about money, and would like to know, I have gained keen insights from real people about women's disposition toward and skills with money. It is clear that girls and young women need more depth to their financial understanding. In essence, one size does not fit all when it comes to financial decision making. True literacy goes a level deeper, teaching people the building blocks of finance and economics, so they can apply principles to different times in their lives, and a range of financial goals.

Hand in hand with the knowledge side of financial literacy is behavior. Disposition has to do with behavior, and skills have to do with knowledge. Both knowledge and behavior are critical when it comes to money management, and believe it or not, that connection can be fairly tenuous. I often compare money to food—even though we know which foods are healthy and nutritious and which are not, we sometimes consciously choose the less healthy version for a multitude of reasons. Similarly with money, even if we know about healthy financial behaviors, we do not always engage in them. Working with real women in addition to analyzing published research helped me better understand what goes into the money knowledge+behavior equation. With this greater understanding, we can better help girls as they move toward adulthood and financial independence.

Another important issue is that unquantifiable, but extremely influential, factor of socialization. How we feel about money and what we know about financial management can be influenced by how money was viewed or treated in the homes of our childhood. Money socialization comes from multiple areas, but our childhood homes are certainly key to providing the foundation. We in turn teach our own children about money, both in what we say and possibly even more importantly, in what we do—or don't do. In order to teach our daughters how to manage money successfully, it is important that we also have the knowledge+behavior to serve as both teachers and powers of example. It is necessary to provide financial education support for parents, as the journey of financially educating one's child is not a journey anyone has to do alone. It is a daunting task, certainly, although the hoped for end result of financial independence is worth the trip.

Money understanding is multifaceted. There's the knowledge that needs to be acquired, and then there are actions that need to be taken. For example, it's not just enough to know that you should be earning what you're worth—you actually have to negotiate the salary. As women earn less, save less, and live longer than men, it is important when investing to take advantage of higher returns, meaning, the money you earn on what you have invested. But this means taking more risk, and women can tend to be risk-averse, which hurts their potential to earn the financial gains required to build a sufficient retirement account.

So it is clear that women can face an extra challenge with taking positive financial actions, as they sometimes conflict with the way we have been socialized, or with what is expected from women in our culture. We have further made the connection that this kind of social learning happens with young girls, and can manifest itself later in women, as a lack of financial advocacy and effectiveness.

So, we have answered the question, why teach girls about money? But the next, logical question is, how?

Teaching financial education to young people can be a challenge, as it can be very abstract to them. The key is making the material interesting or relevant to their lives, and teaching them to engage with and understand complicated concepts. I know from my teaching experience that only can teenagers "get" it; in many cases, they understand financial topics as well as, or even better than, adults. I also know I have an educational approach that works. At the financial and economic education center I founded in western Massachusetts, I effectively taught students how to understand economics, finance, and entrepreneurship. When financial experts visited my classes to give talks to the students, they were frequently impressed with the students' interest and knowledge in finance. "These kids know more than most of my clients!" one stockbroker exclaimed after working with my class.

This book provides a framework for both teaching and learning. It supplies plenty of information about core financial concepts so that parents can feel confident in their own financial understanding. Equally importantly, the book paints a picture of the context around women and money in each chapter to help the adult reader understand how to position the conversation about money as meaningfully as possible. Stories from my work with girls and young women over the past 10 years provide girls' perspectives so adult readers can get a sense of this generation's viewpoint on different financial topics. I provide discussion points to jump-start financial conversations within families and simple but effective experiential exercises at the end of the chapter to further engage and educate the learner.

Equally importantly, this book is designed to fit into the overscheduled lives of American families. Parents do the "heavy lifting" by reading the book and educating themselves on the issues and the content. They can then start financial conversations using the discussion points whenever is convenient—at breakfast, in the car, during family time, or a specially prescribed time to talk about money. Girls can tackle the activities when it fits in their schedules—after school, in the evenings, on weekends, or when they have vacation or some time off.

The book's series of fun and engaging experiential exercises are particularly valuable so girls can learn about money and financial management. We begin by placing the focus squarely on the girls and their lives: What do they want? What are their hopes and dreams? How can they get there? The exercises focus on the present as well as the future, emphasizing what is relevant now and what is important for the future.

The information in the book is easy to follow, and I lay out the following topics that are critical for every adult to understand to be financially successful. But the topics are framed in a way to speak to girls. The topics are laid out in each of the following chapters.

In Chapter 1, as you have read, I provide some general context on women and money, and what that means for the women of tomorrow. The question gets asked and answered: What do our girls need to learn about money now in order to manifest their ambition and dreams—to succeed in the real world—as they grow to adulthood?

The Financial Nutrition® Method comes in to play in Chapter 2—it is the beginning of the answer to the "how" question. The Financial Nutrition® Method provides a foundation for girls to both acquire knowledge and learn behaviors that lead directly to confidence and effectiveness in money management, and educational and career development. The Financial Nutrition® Method looks at things like money having a cost, the quantification of risk, the analysis of value, the understanding of opportunity costs, and the importance of information and experts. These concepts underlie skills development in wealth creation that is so critical for girls and young women today.

In Chapter 3, I show that income is a critical piece—some might argue the most critical piece—of the financial wellness formula. Income can be made through investments, certainly, and we discuss that possibility in Chapter 7. But income through working, or earned income, is how most Americans bring in the majority of their income over a lifetime. As such, the topics covered in this chapter include career planning, salary negotiations, and income potential.

Budgeting and saving are the basis for financial planning, health, and security. In Chapter 4, I explain the difference between needs and wants, and discuss being intentional with money to help combat the societal pressures to spend your money in a certain way. I also talk about goal setting, which is an incredibly powerful tool both in financial management and in life. The idea of spending beyond means is an important lesson when it comes to saving, but it also lays the groundwork for understanding the key economic concept of opportunity cost.

Compounding is where it's at! Seriously. I think so, and Albert Einstein agrees with me. Chapter 5 explains how compound interest is a key factor in borrowing, saving, and investing. But few people understand its incredible power or how it works. In this chapter we do the math—yes the math—and it's not that scary. In this chapter, I discuss how compound interest can dramatically boost the amount of interest repaid on debt held for long periods, especially if the interest rate is high. I also look at how that same compounding power works in your favor when you have money invested and earning a positive return over a long period of time.

Debt can be a friend indeed when one is in need. But young women need a strategy and to be intentional when borrowing money and managing credit. In Chapter 6, I introduce the idea of understanding the value of debt—analyzing whether the costs outweigh the financial benefits and how to keep borrowing costs as low as possible. I also discuss that credit is about trust and that lending institutions use credit scores as a mechanism to determine a borrower's likelihood to repay a loan. I introduce the concept of risk, and how the cost of money, also known as interest rates, reflects perceived risk.

Investing is a hot topic when I teach it to my high school- and college-level classes. These young women come to class knowing bits and pieces about stocks, bonds, and markets, and are very motivated to put all the pieces together and solve this potentially significant wealth-building puzzle. I love teaching girls about investing, as it gets to the heart of financial confidence and engagement. However, investing is an area that I found in my research where women need more education, and I see this to be true in real life. In Chapter 7, I look at what it means to invest, how to invest, and why investing is so important for women.

My goal in Chapter 8 is to help girls understand that taxes don't have to arouse anxiety and fear but are rather a financial output that needs to be considered and managed, whether they are income-based, taxes on investment or inheritance, or capital gains. Understanding how taxes work and planning financial structures strategically to avoid paying more taxes than necessary—including finding meaning through philanthropy—are other ways of being intentional with money. Most importantly, in this chapter I explain that tax planning, and tax preparation, is not something you have to do alone.

Risk is as inevitable as death and taxes. But just like taxes, risk can be managed. As we know, insurance is protection—a hedge against the worst-case scenario. But there's a way to value it, and girls need to grasp this so that they can act in their own best interests. Understanding risk and how to value it is a huge part of being financially literate and successful. Women need to be especially sensitive to issues in pricing with long-term care insurance, given that they live longer and gender-distinct pricing means they pay much more than men. In Chapter 9, I discuss how insurance, including home, auto, long-term care, and life, is protection against financial risk, or a form of risk management. It has a cost and a benefit, and we can figure it out together.

Money can be scary. And happy, sad, shameful, generous, joyful, and empowering. But money is seldom rational—no matter how much we understand its potential—especially when we need it to be. Both scary markets and exciting markets cause people to do silly things, like buy high and sell low. So how can we teach girls to deal with the emotional side of money, and effective financial decision making? In Chapter 10, I provide information about when it makes sense to hire a financial expert as a wealth-building partner and how to choose the right one. I also discuss how ongoing financial education is a key part of the equation, so you know the right questions to ask, and your instinct speaks to you loudly and confidently.

One of the challenges of teaching about money to young women who may not yet have any real financial responsibility is the experiential component. In many cases, young people can only think about managing money abstractly. In Chapter 11 on entrepreneurship, I discuss how starting a small-scale business like a babysitting, tutoring, or pet-care service, and managing the financial processes that go into it, can provide an exciting context for girls to learn how money works. We look at the traits of an entrepreneur, social versus for-profit ventures, and the steps to starting a business. This information is particularly engaging to girls as I am finding that more and more young women are actually interested in starting their own enterprise, whether it is for-profit or socially based, which reflects the rising trend among women entrepreneurs.

Once you have laid the foundation for financial understanding with conversations and our Financial Nutrition® discussion and activities, it is time to start some real-life experience. I provide some examples in Chapter 12 ranging in complexity and scope: they include starting a for-profit or social enterprise, opening an IRA and tracking its performance, getting a job or managing an allowance to learn how to deal with actual money, setting goals for longer-term purchases to practice budgeting, and deciding between needs and wants. These ideas are meant to bring theoretical learning into the practical world, and in my experience, few exercises are more thrilling for a young girl than those that demonstrate a growing mastery over money.

Appendix 1 provides a comprehensive framework for girls to start Financial Nutrition® clubs at school. This book emphasizes economic empowerment, and girls starting clubs on their own is a great first step toward independence. In addition, clubs provide a community where everyone can help each other and learn together. The Financial Nutrition® clubs can include research and discussion around topics like the gender wage gap, and projects to do together like starting a new venture, or looking for jobs. Appendix 2 provides information about the Financial Nutrition® curriculum that can be used for a class at school. The curriculum addresses the topics around the context of women and money, income and salary negotiations, budgeting, compound interest, debt and credit, and banking services.

Financial Nutrition® strives to create and inspire a baseline sense of financial competence, confidence, and priority, showing that managing money is as critical a skill as managing social media, with far reaching consequence. We offer opportunities for learning, doing, and moving forward on the path of financial independence. This gift of the path to financial independence and success is, I believe, one of the best gifts we can give to the girls in our lives.

CHAPTER TWO

The Financial Nutrition®
Method Underlying It All

Introduction

So it's pretty clear that girls need financial literacy—both knowledge and behavior—but there are certain challenges involved. First, there's getting the financial education, as many schools do not offer personal finance classes, and families are not always comfortable talking about money. And then there's the behavior. Money behavior does not always make sense and can be impacted negatively by emotions and socialization, in addition to a lack of knowledge. And hanging over all of this is the fact that most teenagers do not typically have occasion or need to manage their own money, and financial life, so there is not as much opportunity for learning by doing. So to most young people, money management is a fairly abstract concept, without a lot of opportunity for experiential learning, or financial education, of any kind.

The critical need for women's financial literacy comes from important factors like the fact that women make less money than men but outlive them by at least five years and end their lives with less cumulative savings.[1] This economic disadvantage means that women really needed to have solid financial understanding, as well as economic empowerment. But other statistics are being bandied about that make an even stronger case for the engagement of girls and women around money. For one, women currently control 51 percent of wealth in the United States and may control as much as two-thirds of it by the year 2020, according to Forbes.[2] So in order for women of the future to understand how to manage their substantial asset base effectively, we need to think about how to engage girls around money now.

Girls need to learn how to analyze the evolving financial landscape, their options within it, and how to plan for their hopes and dreams whether they involve career, family, or both. We can teach our daughters that they can do anything they want—they just need to understand the economics of their decision so they can take care of themselves and their families financially and have the freedom to live their lives in the way they choose. It's important to teach girls about money now so they can make informed choices in the future as the trend for women's financial responsibility— and possibility—grows.

The Financial Nutrition® Method that I developed from my work in finance, my research into women's financial literacy including disposition and behaviors, and my experience teaching teenaged girls about money addresses both financial knowledge and behavior. Voicing an opinion, fighting for a salary, knowing and articulating your worth, and working effectively with financial services professionals are all keys to taking care of oneself and gaining financial independence and stability. The Financial Nutrition® Method provides a unique approach to engage girls to both acquire knowledge and learn behaviors that lead directly to confidence and effectiveness in money management, and educational and career development.

Genesis of the Method

I learned from my unique experience as teacher, researcher, mother, and woman, the societal and cultural messages around money and worth, and the societal expectations of girls, and how these factors can combine and eventually lead to financial disempowerment and disengagement in women. On an education and knowledge level, in my research I connected the financial dots, discovering the key areas women need to understand and manifest in order to holistically grow wealth and develop financial independence, and how that learning—and eventual behavior— can be hampered by the disempowering and destructive societal messages we send to girls.

The Financial Nutrition® Method provides the solution to the problem of women's financial inequality by demonstrating that economic power is not just about knowledge and information; it's also about learned, socialized behavior. It makes the connection between the hard and soft information—the knowledge and the socialized behavior—and how to teach the integrated version to girls. It addresses the connection between issues like salary negotiations for grown women, and girls being taught not to "brag"—which ultimately can contribute to the stubborn, entrenched 78 percent pay gap. It deals with the connection between teaching girls to "play it safe" and risk aversion when it comes to investing—which can ultimately yield a failure to invest in assets that grow wealth and provide security in retirement.

I discovered early on that the key to helping girls learn about money was to create actual "experiences" for learning, otherwise known as experiential learning. Experiential money learning is effective for a number of reasons. First, it's engaging, which means it holds attention in subjects that may not otherwise seem relevant, or even interesting. It can involve activities, acting, and great discussions. Second, it's effective. The engagement that comes through the experience means that learning happens at a deeper level, and knowledge is integrated. Finally, it gets to the heart of the dispositional issues with girls. We've already talked a lot about how socialization can hold women back financially, and that behavior link starts with girls. Experiential learning can help build confidence, competence, and positive behaviors in financial areas where women typically struggle.

The knowledge piece is also a big one here. Even when financial management is taught, it can be superficial, with a one-size-fits-all approach. Interestingly, financial literacy can be viewed in lots of different ways. Is it enough just to know that debt is bad, or is it better to have a foundation of understanding that helps you analyze when debt might be a positive thing in your life, and who you might consult with to get additional information on the issue? Finance comes from economics, and true money learning is rife with economic concepts like opportunity costs, cost-benefit analysis, and psychic benefits. Knowing these deeper economic concepts means you can apply financial behaviors more specifically and effectively to your own life. A deeper understanding of what is really happening in a financial analysis is critical for money learning, especially for a population that is starting out behind in the game.

Looking at all of these issues, I have developed a pedagogical system that encapsulates what is needed to effectively educate girls about money. The Financial Nutrition® Method is a unique approach to teaching girls about money. The pedagogy involves knowledge acquisition and skills development, as well as critical work around disposition toward money. Through teaching foundational concepts of finance and economics, as well as practical applications, students become confident and well versed in their understanding of money and the financial system. Knowledge leads to confidence, and confidence is critical both in terms of risk taking, but also in learning to trust your instinct. Instruction in the area of entrepreneurship involves the key elements of entrepreneurial thinking—creative analysis, idea generation, opportunity recognition, and goal setting—that are important work and life skills in the new economy. The Financial Nutrition® Method provides a foundation for girls to both acquire knowledge and behavior, resulting in confidence in money management, and educational and career development.

Experiential Learning

Experiential learning, in a sense, utilizes a sort of "lab" approach to learn by doing. Entrepreneurship education is a perfect example of an effective approach in this area. As girls and young women work on developing companies, they utilize a broad range of financial tools and skills, and that learning occurs at a much deeper level both because of the engagement and the experience of working with financial issues. The new venture development provides both the context, and the means, to actively engage in financial analysis and decision making, integrating financial learning at a deeper level.

Experiential learning is particularly effective when employed by addressing "real life" issues. For example, learning about budgeting when you are actually earning money and have seemingly unattainable savings goals provides an incentive to both learn, and practice, the new information and skill. In this way, experiential learning not only helps knowledge acquisition at a deeper level, but in an area like financial management that involves taking actions, it provides the experience of taking the actions that you are learning about. In this way, experiential learning can have a direct impact on financial behavior, as the behavior is practiced as part of the learning process and knowledge acquisition.

Socialization

Socialized behaviors in girls can be a contributing factor to future economic disempowerment and perceived financial illiteracy of women. For example, it's not just enough to know that you should be earning what you're worth; you actually have to stand up for yourself, articulate your worth, and negotiate your salary. Encouraging girls to be nice, well behaved, and considerate of other people's feelings over their own might make them "nice" girls, but it also promotes behaviors that in the future could hurt them economically. Girls may learn that it is important to be liked, to not be bossy, and to not make a scene. Girls may learn, in preparation of possible eventual motherhood, that taking care of others means sacrificing themselves. Learning to devalue yourself at a young age can have a direct impact later in life on how you negotiate a salary, or articulate your worth—or more likely in not negotiating a salary, given that 70 percent of women actually do not negotiate a salary.[3] In the workplace, this is a behavior that can cost you hundreds of thousands over a lifetime.[4] Because of cultural messaging, girls can face an uphill battle when it comes to growing up to be women with positive money behaviors.

Financial learning that addresses socialized behaviors can mean a couple of things. First, there is the teaching of the context of these behaviors—discussing openly how girls feel about themselves, how they feel about speaking up, and whether they are able to recognize or articulate their own value. Next, there is the connection of those ideas and behaviors with future financial behaviors, and providing a learning path that connects the two, and teaches more financially positive behaviors. For example, before you can effectively negotiate a salary or a raise, you need to recognize and articulate your value so you can make an effective argument. It may be that for some girls—and later for women—value recognition and self-promotion does not come naturally. So part of the educational process to teach girls about income maximization and how to negotiate a salary is first teaching them how to recognize strengths in themselves and articulate those strengths to themselves and others.

Knowledge = Confidence

The Financial Nutrition® Method teaches the elemental building blocks of financial literacy, like interest rates and the cost of money, as well as money skills and behaviors, like budgeting. The pedagogy interweaves financial information and economic concepts so that a deeper understanding is possible. This deeper understanding means that students will eventually be able to be more proactive in their financial lives, applying their financial understanding effectively to different life cycles, financial challenges, and financial opportunities.

This broad knowledge and comprehension can also lead to a greater confidence in financial management. For real confidence in money management, full comprehension of these underlying concepts, like the cost of money, is key to being able to engage in successful financial behaviors. Additionally, when working with financial professionals, you can feel confident asking questions, and self-advocating, which is not always the case for women. And with this, the possibility of leading a life of financial independence and success on your own terms can become a reality.

Key Concepts

The Financial Nutrition® Method involves five key ideas, with component concepts to further articulate the ideas. The five key ideas include:

- Money as commodity
- Risk
- Value
- Opportunity costs
- Information

These ideas are important as we teach girls about money, utilizing techniques that impact knowledge, behavior, and socialization. The five key ideas can be understood as follows.

Money Has a Cost (Money as Commodity)

Component concepts:

- Interest
- Compound interest
- Rate of return
- Time value of money
- Debt/credit

Money has a cost, plain and simple. The cost of money is known as interest, and interest, particularly compound interest, is a key element in credit, debt, saving, and investing. The cost of money also comes into play in more complicated financial topics like rate of return, which is a calculation of earnings from an investment. The cost of money is similarly a factor in the concept of the time value of money, which involves the potential earning rate of money, meaning that money received sooner has more value because of its earning potential if put effectively to work. Money is a commodity because it can be used, at a cost, as an input to earn more money, or create opportunity.

Although some of these ideas, like rate of return and time value of money, seem like concepts that would only be grappled with in a business school classroom or in the conference rooms of high finance, the reality is all of these elements of the idea of money having a cost are critical to decision making about how to use money. These decisions could be simple like whether to make a purchase, or more complicated, like whether to borrow a lot of money or to put money into investments. It is easy to see as well how the cost of money factors in to financial behaviors like budgeting.

The idea of a money as a commodity is an important one, in part because we give money so much meaning through our emotional connection or reaction to it. As we know, money can mean a lot of different things to different people, but at the end of the day, money truly is a means of exchange, plain and simple. Money can be used to invest in the future, it can be used to provide for your family in the present, it can be used for opportunity and security. How you use your money can have a great impact in the life that you are able to lead. Understanding that money is available to work for you is a critical understanding when learning how to manage money proactively.

Risk Can and Should Be Quantified (Risk)

Component concepts:

- Risk management
- Insurance
- Investing
- Creditworthiness

Risk is the possibility that something bad will happen. With investing, risk means the possibility of losing some or all of your original investment. Risk can be scary, for sure, and it can be easy to just choose to avoid it all together. But while investments with low risk may not have far to fall, their stability also typically means they do not have far to climb. This means you do not have the same potential to make money. Think, buy low—sell high.

So for women who earn less, save less, and live longer than men, it is so important when investing to take advantage of higher returns, meaning, the money you earn on what you have invested. And while it is impossible to manage away all the risk in any portfolio because markets are too unpredictable, there are approaches that can help mitigate risk. Even so, a certain amount of risk is necessary in order to earn returns that can grow the type of wealth we will all need in retirement.

Confidence comes from having a plan, but it also comes from knowing there are protections in place. Managing risk is all about having the right insurance, careful tax planning, investing for different life phases and priorities, and having savings and other financial cushions in place for unexpected financial and family difficulties.

Value Has Multiple Applications (Value)

Component concepts:

- Monetary value
- Psychic value
- Investment value
- Cost-benefit analysis

Value has so many meanings with money and even more in life. Value is all about relative comparisons—does one thing have more worth to you than something else? But at the end of the day, value is really about what is important to you and what you want to get out of life. Monetary value is a similarly easy concept to understand. What does something cost, and is it worth it? In terms of an investment, will it yield more in the future than it does today? Monetary value and investment value are connected in that way. An investment looks at future value, which none of us can know absolutely. Monetary value is the value of money in the here and now.

Psychic value is an important kind of value, because it's about happiness. Although something may not make you rich, it might still make you happy. You can take a job that you love, even if it pays less than one you hate. You may find value in taking time off to raise kids, or pursue life as an artist, or travel for a year. This would commonly be known as psychic value. Cost-benefit analysis comes into play with the value analysis. Is the outcome worth what you put into it, and is that scenario better than another one? What is the benefit at the end of the day, related to the cost?

The idea of value and cost-benefit analysis are critical pieces of the job and salary negotiation puzzle. It may be that you are not able to negotiate the salary you want, but the job has value nevertheless, either because you love the work or it is a stepping-stone to something even better.

Opportunity Costs (Opportunity)

Component concepts:

- Income potential
- Goal setting
- Tax planning

The cost of money is also related to a critical economic concept known as opportunity cost. Opportunity cost is a general term that can be applied to many things besides money. But in the case of money, an opportunity cost is the fact that the same money can only be spent on one thing at a time. So, money spent on a trip to Europe cannot then be used as the down payment for a house. Opportunity costs are the costs of the alternatives not chosen.

Goals are a key motivator in many areas of life—athletics, careers, and not least of all, money. Among other things, goals provide an incentive, and an intentional option, when we want to give in to something that is easier, more fun, or less painful. Goal setting also comes in handy too when dealing with the economic issue of opportunity costs. Savings goals foster more intentional spending, meaning, they provide a framework to prevent losing an opportunity to buy something important down the road by spending it on less important things in the short term.

This idea of spending beyond means is an important lesson when it comes to saving, but it also lays the groundwork for understanding this key economic concept of opportunity costs. By spending more than one earns, the savings goal moves further away. We don't always have a choice of when we need to spend money. But it is a great thing to understand opportunity costs at a young age when the stakes are a little lower. For adult women, an opportunity cost might involve losing out on owning a home or saving early for retirement. Young women who learn this concept as teenagers will be one step ahead in financial know-how and as adults will better understand how to seize opportunities to their economic advantage.

Information as a Resource (Information)

Component concepts:

- Education
- Advisers
- Resources
- Information asymmetry

It's important to know the market and understand the economy so that you can trust your instinct when it comes to investing. However, you do not have to be an expert. We all have our areas of expertise, and you don't have to be an expert in all things. But if you're not an investment expert, you may want to work with someone who is. When you do look for an expert, find one who provides what you need—a style that is comfortable for you and all the information you want. This relationship is a very important one, so make sure you feel good about it, and don't hire someone until you do.

Education and engagement with your money in all areas is critical. For investing, it is important to make sure you educate yourself on an ongoing basis, including self-education through books and media, or formal education through classes, or working closely with and learning from an expert. Engagement means monitoring your money, the markets, and the economy, and staying in touch with your financial adviser if you have one. It's important to understand what is happening in the world and how it is impacting your money and financial security.

Salary negotiations are a brilliant example of the economic concept of *information asymmetry*—an obvious imbalance of power because one side has information the other side does not—as they are seldom transparent. For example, most negotiators do not disclose what other members of the company are being paid, how much they really have available to spend on the position, and the factors in the calculation of employee value. This information and understanding is key to providing financial education to young women that ends the gender wage gap, and empowers women to earn the income they deserve, and need, to take care of themselves.

CHAPTER THREE

Income: Learn Not to Underearn

Introduction

If someone told you that you could earn an extra half a million dollars over your lifetime by doing the job you were already planning to do, what would you say? Well, studies show that a half a million dollars is what underne-gotiating a first salary can cost someone by age 60.[1] And this is not just a problem from decades past, when women in the workplace were still a novelty. Recent women college graduates continue to undernegotiate their first salaries by an average of over $5,000 per year, while median salaries right out of college are only around $35,000.[2] Despite all the advances we keep hearing about for women in the United States today, they continue to earn less, save less, live longer, and take increasing financial responsibility for their families. So how can we break this cycle for the next generation of young women?

Women continue to earn a fraction of what their male counterparts do—coming in at 78 cents on the dollar in 2013, according to the U.S. Census Bureau.[3] Although President Kennedy signed into law the Equal Pay Act of 1963, and women have seen greater pay equity since that time, pay gains have stagnated in the past few years.[4] And that gender pay gap is accompanied by other trends that provide barriers to women earning what they are worth. More and more women are entering the U.S. workforce, and make up about half of it now, but hold far fewer leadership positions than men. The United States is still one of the only countries in the world without paid maternity leave, and some studies show a woman loses 4 percent of her salary with each child she has.[5] By some accounts, the income discrepancies women face can cost them $1.2 million over a lifetime.[6]

Sometimes by choice, sometimes out of necessity, women are most likely to bear primary responsibility for child care and elder care, which means they may be in and out of the workforce, cutting into the momentum of their careers, taking positions and projects that are "off the radar" to create more flexibility in their work lives. Some women may want a more linear career, with a straight upward trajectory, and may be able to put as much time and effort into it as necessary. Those at the top 10 percent tend to see more equal pay and opportunity in the workplace, which translates into higher incomes, higher lifetime savings, lower debt, and sufficient savings for retirement. But the women who take a less linear path—moving in and out of the workforce for child care or elder care, changing fields, trying to work part-time at various times of life—are likely to be penalized for it economically.

And those of us who are fighting for the top jobs may not truly be able to compete if we are not completely willing to sacrifice our time and personal lives. Research from Harvard labor economist Claudia Goldin shows that gender-based income disparity happens *within* industries—meaning, it's not always the case that women are choosing jobs with lower pay and greater flexibility, like teachers compared to surgeons, but they are getting paid less for the same jobs. Goldin's conclusion is that firms reward people who can work longer hours and sacrifice more personal time.[7] This type of commitment to a job tends to eliminate the possibility for flexibility and plain old time at home, which women with families almost invariably want or require.

Income is a critical piece—some might argue the most critical piece—of the financial wellness formula. Although controlling spending is an important part of the equation, some expenses can only go so low. Adult financial obligations like paying a mortgage, paying off student loans, providing for a family, saving for retirement, plus scores of "unforeseen circumstances," are unavoidable.

Income can be earned through investments, certainly, and we discuss that possibility in Chapter 7. But income through working is how most Americans make the majority of their money. As such, one of the most important areas I focus on in my Financial Nutrition® teaching is how to maximize income and effectively negotiate salaries. Information about how to make this puzzle piece work is critical for girls who can expect to face financial challenges as adults, and who will—wittingly or not—be making significant financial decisions, like career direction, in the next few years.

Happily, understanding the landscape for income maximization can be taught starting at a young age.

Of course, this work may seem to come with its own set of challenges. Many teenaged girls do not have much financial responsibility, so learning how to maximize income (for a job they don't yet have in a career they've not yet settled on) may not seem extremely relevant. They may not know how to research potential jobs and salaries, and young people do not typically understand how salary negotiations work. Some girls may have difficulty articulating their value or even seeing it for themselves. So where do you start?

The key to helping girls grow into women who are prepared to effectively take responsibility for their income is to start coaching them when they are young on how to recognize and articulate their value and advocate on behalf of themselves, in any context.

Financial Nutrition® Method: Value and Opportunity

- Money as commodity
- Risk
- *Value*
- *Opportunity costs*
- Information

Value has so many meanings: Monetary value is about what something costs and its worth, whereas psychic value is about happiness. With money, the value is in how much of it you have, and sometimes money does not buy happiness. In the context of income, it is important to look at what has value for you. Although financial security is of paramount importance, a job that pays less but provides financial security and happiness may have more value for you than a job that pays more but is not something you want to do. You may find value in life pursuits that don't provide income but are much more important to you, like being a stay-at-home mother.

Value also comes into play in the context of income when you determine how much you should get paid. The analysis for what a salary pays involves a number of factors, including what a person is willing to take in compensation. However, one of the important factors is the value you add in the work that you are doing. Frequently there are elements of this analysis that are subjective, but some are not, and we will examine these factors more in this chapter.

Opportunity costs comes into play with the analysis of value with income. A job can have value for you for purely monetary reasons, meaning, it pays you what you need and what you think you are worth. However, a job may not pay you want you think it should, which is in a sense a cost, but the job could be necessary to building the career that you want and getting you to where you want to be in the future. In that way, although the lower-paying job has a cost, it also has a value. The opportunity costs analysis can help you decide just how many costs—and value—different job and salary options have.

Girls Already Struggle with Life Choices

When I work with young women in high school and college, it is clear that they are already thinking a lot about their lives as adults, and many of them have ambitious career goals. I talk to young girls who aspire to run Fortune 500 companies, practice medicine in underserved areas, and launch high profile legal careers. But along with those big plans comes a measure of anxiety, and even resignation. Some of these young women are already completely stressed out trying to envision their adult lives with work, graduate school, and motherhood—and worrying about how to time everything, and still be able to have kids, be successful, and be a good mother who is there for her children. They wonder how to maintain a loving marriage but still earn enough independent income in case the partnership falls apart. These young women are trying to figure out a puzzle that preceding generations of women have not yet solved. Some of the issues have to do with the limitations of the space-time continuum— you can't be in a full-time job or graduate program and also be a full-time stay-at-home mom. That's a physics problem to which there is no obvious solution.

Concerned as my students may be by the challenge of "having it all," their actual understanding of the role money plays in life is limited. I often see a disconnect in young women's expectations for their lives and the income they will need to live their dreams. I recall one group of young college women I taught who were commendably idealistic and well meaning in their hopes for the future. Many wanted to work in not-for-profits and help those less fortunate, and live in New York City or San Francisco, the two most expensive cities in the United States.[8] They had no idea of the types of salaries they might earn in the not-for-profit world or the cost of living in their city of choice, and some of the students were graduating and headed into the "real world" in the next few months. I did not criticize their life choices, but we worked together to determine what kind of income they would need to support the lifestyle they imagined. It was an incredibly valuable and eye-opening exercise for these students.

With college debt surpassing $1 trillion in the United States,[9] the reality of the need to graduate college with an earning capacity to pay off student loans, as well as pay for regular life expenses and start saving for retirement, is critical for the young women I teach. These women are entering a world that is not kind economically to the younger generations. Studies show that adults under 35 currently have a savings rate of –2 percent.[10] Millennials are having a hard time saving because for 47 percent of them, their monthly debt level consumes half their paycheck.[11] With financial literacy among millennials pretty universally low, these young women (and their younger sisters) need the knowledge and the tools to take care of themselves financially.

My goal in teaching girls financial understanding and money management skills is not to scare the students, or nudge them into certain life choices about work and family. Rather, I am trying to give them a sense of the issues they may face, and thereafter, the financial tools they need to derive as many options as possible in order to achieve their hopes, dreams, and lifestyle of choice. I work with them to figure out solutions to the barriers they may face as adult women, by giving them information about the highest-paying college majors, and helping them see that their early career choices—perhaps based on their major—can be a key economic decision. We also discuss salary differentials in the fields that women typically don't enter and begin to see the possibilities in those less sought after areas, like STEM-related fields. Income maximization and job negotiations are other key elements that I cover in my "live-your-dreams" approach to financial understanding.

Why do these young women already feel stymied about their possible life choices? Those who want a family are afraid that staying home with their children for a measure of time will impact their ability to be successful in their careers, or to even have meaningful careers. Some are afraid not to have financial independence, as they may know women who were left in vulnerable positions after a divorce or a spouse's death. Aware of the concept of a "biological clock," some are already grappling with family timing concerns when they think about embarking on extensive graduate study like medicine or doctoral work. And this generation of young women is ambitious. According to the Pew Research Center, 66 percent of women 18–34 say being successful in a high-paying career or profession is "one of the most important things" or "very important" in their lives, compared to 59 percent of men in the same age group.[12] I see that ambition reflected in the younger girls with whom I work, and I also see their concern about what could happen to them if they don't have a career and an income of their own.

Unfortunately, these concerns sound shockingly similar to those that my friends and I shared when we first began thinking of having families, some 20 or so years ago—before girls were outperforming boys in school, before women's ambition levels surpassed men, before we knew how to "lean in." These decisions are so difficult for all of our generations because they are not just economic decisions—they are social and emotional decisions as well. We battle what society and our family tells us we should do, the compromises we might need to make with a partner, our own desires and life goals, and the responsibilities life gives us. Managing the income side of the equation effectively can provide women with some additional (and sorely needed) opportunity and flexibility in these life decisions.

Trends in Women's Income Inequality and Challenges

So while the gender wage gap has persisted stubbornly over the past 20 years, what *has* changed?

Women's academic performance is an area that screams equality—or even superiority. Women now outperform men in higher education with more women going to college than men.[13] But even though women are outperforming men, their representation in leadership positions has not kept pace. We still see a "leadership ambition gap." In her bestselling book *Lean In*, Facebook executive Sheryl Sandberg cites a McKinsey study of more than four thousand employers of leading companies that found that 36 percent of men wanted to reach the C-suite, compared to only 18 percent of the women.[14] This is in contrast to the statistics that show strong ambition in women ages 16–34. Although women's talent is clearly as high as men's, their diminishing ambition for the highest-paying jobs holds them back from achieving high levels of income.

To this end, it's critical to understand what data goes in to that all-important median 78 cents on the dollar statistic, and how it all plays out when the data is disaggregated. Pew Research Center research does a beautiful job of showing where the biggest income discrepancies for women are by breaking the data down by age group.

The data tells the story of the earnings wage gap on a generational basis, and over time. Through time, from 1979 to 2010, women's earnings as a percentage of men's have risen. It is also clear that certain age groups—like women between the ages of 16–24—are closer to parity than others, like those between the ages of 55–64.[15] When I discuss these trends with the young women in my classes, we talk about what might be at the root of these differences. These savvy young women can dissect and interpret the data effectively, citing the following issues:

1. The jobs that 16–24-year-olds have are more menial, so there is less room for salary bumps and negotiations.
2. Older women in the 45–54 and 55–64 ranges are likely victims of early discrimination, which is why their earning gap is higher, and has changed less since 2010.
3. The women entering the workforce more recently, like those in the 25–34 range and the 35–44 range, have benefited from greater equality trends.

My students are bright and aware, and they get that information all right. But what I have had to explain to them is about another critical point in the 35–44 and 45–54 age ranges—these are the ages when professional women may be more likely to have kids, leave the workforce, or opt to follow a career path where they do not—for whatever reason—seek the big money for the big job. But those are also the years when working people typically come into their own professionally, start to make more money, and move up the ladder. But it appears that women in these age groups lean *out* just at the time when they have the greatest career opportunity to lean *in*.

The career and income cycle for women is a fairly complex one, and rife with economic and family obligations, society dictates, and forces that are not about money, but are about psychic value, or what makes a person happy. Although some women may not *have* to work when they have kids, they may still want to. Conversely, some women who could work may want to stay home and raise their children. Whatever option a woman chooses, she is almost always economically penalized when it comes to caring for others.

Nancy Folbre, a MacArthur fellowship–winning economist, discusses this "care penalty." According to Folbre, women who take time off to take care of family members gain less work experience and earn less money than men with the same levels of education. A married housewife is compensated through receiving a share of the income her husband earns, which leaves her vulnerable if the marriage ends or her husband dies.[16] Statistics show that being a mother tends to lower women's earnings even if they don't take time off from the workforce. In fact, the more children a woman has, the less she earns, even if she works the same amount of time with one employer as a woman with no children.[17]

A similar situation occurs with elder care. The National Center for Women and Aging at Brandeis University and the National Alliance of

Caregivers' research reported that two-thirds of people providing more than eight hours a week in unpaid care for elderly relatives missed out at work by forgoing promotions and training. As it happens, three-fourths of all home caregivers for the elderly are women. Women tend to take more personal responsibility for their children and other dependents, according to Folbre.[18]

Although it may look right now that women are destined to live their lives in a financial catch-22, the fact that women face the economic barriers they do is exactly why it is important to teach girls about income maximization. It is important, first of all, to understand which factors impact income. As most parents know, education is one important element, both in terms of how much education a person has and in what area. All college degrees are not created equal in terms of earning potential.

The Education-Income Analysis

Helping girls to understand the relationship between income and education means asking a lot of questions like: which kinds of jobs pay more, which kinds pay less, and are women pursuing any certain type? For example, there are still more female teachers and retail workers, and more male engineers and surgeons. Why, I ask my students, do you suppose that is? Do certain jobs require a specific major, and which majors tend to lead to better paying jobs? Are there certain jobs that tend to be more flexible in terms of hours, or other jobs that will require a great deal of time and sacrifice in order to get ahead? Knowing the answers to these questions can help young women figure out how to make sure their income supports their lifestyle, and ultimately, their dreams.

First of all, data shows that a college education and advanced professional and graduate degrees have a huge impact on average income for women and men alike. This data shows a positive income trend for women given how well women are performing in academic venues.

But while women are excelling academically and are clearly entering the workforce in greater numbers than ever before, according to a recent report by the Center for Research on Gender in the Professions at UC San Diego, women are still underrepresented in the three industries the report examined: law, medicine, and science and technology. Women make up only 21 percent of scientists and engineers employed in business and industry. In medicine, women make up only 34 percent of physicians.[19] And it is these STEM-related jobs that pay the most directly out of college, according to the *Wall Street Journal*.[20] Women now make up about half of the overall workforce, but estimates show that only 23 percent of workers in STEM-related fields are women. Despite some recent news about women in top tech jobs, the dearth of women in science, engineering, and technology is a persistent problem, and avoiding STEM-related fields can impact income.

Why are relatively few women working in STEM-related fields? The causes are multiple: Girls who feel underconfident in math and science may choose to avoid those subjects in school, which likely means veering away from STEM majors in college that might ultimately lead to a higher-paying job. Some of the issues may be cultural, for example in technology, which purportedly has a frat-boy "brogrammer" culture that women may not feel comfortable with. Another issue is social—with fewer women in STEM-related fields, there are fewer role models for girls, and fewer sign-posts to follow.

Some research suggests that the most important factor in women's belief in their ability to succeed in STEM-related fields is the confidence that significant others—including parents and teachers—showed in the women's capabilities.[21] In another study, Stanford University Professor Carol Dweck asked the question, "Why aren't more of our brightest females pursuing careers in math and science?" Her research findings show that the messages girls hear in educational settings about math ability being "a gift negatively impacts their ability to perform in the subject." When females got the message that math skills are developed and not inherent, their performance was equal to their male counterparts. The "gift" mentality creates a vulnerability in girls that can lead to a lack of confidence and underperformance in math.[22] So it's clear that how we talk to girls about math and other STEM subjects, and *our* belief in their abilities, is critical to their interest in and performance in those fields.

Going into a STEM-related field is not the only option for leveraging education into a career that creates wealth and financial independence. One approach to higher earnings in low-paying postcollege fields is graduate work. According to Georgetown University's Center on Education and the Workforce, a graduate degree can increase median lifetime earnings in some fields by over 50 percent compared to a bachelor's degree in the same field.[23] Starting a successful company—while no mean feat—can be another way to develop tremendous earning potential regardless of major or degree, and it has the added advantage for women entrepreneurs of no externally created "glass ceiling" for income.

But no matter which major they choose or career path they follow, girls need to understand that the gender pay gap is a real issue, and they need to learn how to take care of their own salary maximization.

Job Negotiations: A Crucial Lesson

One way to deal with the income gap that girls will face is to acquaint them with the notion of salary negotiations early on. Negotiating and other forms of self-advocacy do not come naturally to everyone, so helping foster the skill and mindset at an early age can mean the difference between wealth and opportunity and a life with far less. Teaching our girls to recognize and articulate their own value is a lesson that will serve them well in every aspect of their lives.

When I teach teenaged girls about money and financial management, the "Income" lesson is one of my favorite classes, because so many of the factors that impact women and money become very clear in the guileless responses of these young women. We talk about the studies that show that recent female college graduates are undernegotiating their male counterparts in their first jobs out of college.

In one recent class, I had an initial conversation about the students' ideas of their financial worth in the workplace and pointed out that their male peers were likely to out-negotiate them in their entry-level jobs. As they contemplated the topic of salary negotiations, their reactions revealed some interesting—and telling—insights. Many girls voiced concerns about asking for more. One young woman said she felt that she was the one who should sacrifice and not ask for more money as it could hurt the company or other people working there. Another young woman said she would never ask for a raise; she would expect her hard work to speak for itself. These responses were similar to ones I'd been hearing from girls for years and also align with some I have heard from women who were already in the midst of their careers. In the class, we talked as a group about why these kinds of attitudes were bound to maintain the gender wage gap. We talked about how you don't need to sacrifice when you are getting paid to do a job and that you should be paid what you are worth. We also talked about how financial interests between employer and employee are rarely aligned, and waiting for an employer to give you a raise might mean never getting one.

I typically follow the discussion with an exercise I like to call "Just Say No." The goal of this exercise is to give young women experience advocating for themselves financially, and practice turning down salary offers that did not match their target income goal. In this simulation, students researched the salary level for a job they might like to do one day and then paired up to negotiate starting salaries. Students took turns playing the role of employer and employee. The "employer" was supposed to make a salary offer to the "employee" that was below the salary level for the position. The "employee" students were instructed to refuse the first offer they were given by their partner and then present reasons, based on their experience and research about the position and the market for the job, why they should be paid more than the proffered starting salary.

I have done this exercise many times with students, and invariably the young women complain that they find it difficult or unnatural to ask for more money, even if they have the experience and research to back up their request. But these same students *also* tell me that the act of asking for what they are worth—and frequently receiving a higher salary as a result—is liberating and empowering.

Salary negotiations are also a brilliant example of an opportunity to teach about the economic concept of *information asymmetry*—an obvious imbalance of power—as both sides of the table do not have the same information, and job negotiations are seldom transparent. For example, most negotiators do not disclose what other members of the company are being paid, how much they really have to spend on the position, and the factors in the calculation of employee value. Thus, I teach my students that in negotiating a salary, research is a critical piece, and that knowing what a job should pay is necessary before entering the negotiation.

Do Try This at Home!

But for these behavioral lessons on salary negotiations to really stick, we need to go a little deeper. It's important to talk to girls about articulating their worth, or the positive points of "bragging" from the time they are young.

Start with questions like: *What do you want in life? What are your hopes and dreams? What do you need to do to achieve them?* If girls are stumped at what they might be interested in doing for a job one day, or even what they are good at now—as many girls seem to be—the "What Am I Good At?" exercise can help reset the "no bragging" mindset and help girls understand and articulate their strengths.

Here is how the "What Am I Good At?" exercise works in three easy steps:

- Take out a small notebook.
- Each night before going to sleep, write down three things you did really well that day. This can be anything from acing a math test, to helping a friend with a problem, to doing good work at a part-time job or internship.
- Every couple of months, review the daily entries in the notebook, and think about the trends and themes that you see. Write down any recurring themes.

This simple daily action can help create a muscle and mindset for owning and articulating your strengths and talents. The understanding gained from the activity can be joined eventually with other questions like "What is your passion?" and "What does your community need?" and "What aligns your interests?" when determining a college major or a career choice. In fact, this exercise is effective at any age, from girl onto adult.

Knowing your strengths and keeping track of your accomplishments is also an important tool in negotiating a salary or asking for a raise or a promotion. This articulation of worth and the value one brings to an organization is a key element in income discussions. Articulating your worth and value is also important when working part-time as a teenager or trying to secure an internship or a leadership position in a club. In school, good performance is automatically rewarded and there is a clear-cut system to monitor achievement. But in the workplace, performance and achievements may be less visible to the people who control salaries, so it is essential to learn how to describe your value and contributions.

The opportunity we have with girls is to teach them to understand and articulate their self-worth from a young age so they never have to unlearn devaluing themselves. Basic training on negotiations is always good advice. If we teach girls these ideas and behaviors early on, they will not make the mistake of undernegotiating their first job—or any job—and the seemingly impossible, entrenched, gender wage gap will finally close. These skills and habits also apply to women, so even if you are deep into your career, it's never too late to learn how to maximize your salary potential with these simple steps.

Discussion Points

Here are some additional discussion points you can share with the young woman in your life about how to self-advocate, successfully negotiate salaries, and ultimately recognize her own worth. Financial conversations using these discussion points can be had whenever is convenient—at breakfast, in the car, during family time, or a specially prescribed time to talk about money in a group or a club.

1. *Know your market.* It is critical to go into a salary negotiation knowing what the job generally pays. This way, you can avoid undervaluing yourself, but will also avoid asking for a number that is so unrealistically high that you lose credibility. If the overall economy and job market are poor, this will reflect on the market, and you may have less leverage to negotiate a higher salary. But knowing what the job pays is a key piece of information, no matter how strong the job market is that

year. This research can be done online and by talking to people who work in the industry.

2. *Know your worth.* Understand how your background, skills, and knowledge add value to that particular position, and that specific organization, so you can articulate it in the negotiation. Knowing your worth pertains to entry-level positions as well as higher-level ones. Women are often taught to sacrifice and be caretakers. Although these human traits are important for family and society, at the negotiating table they can mean not achieving a salary or a promotion that you deserve.

3. *Understand your interests are not aligned.* Think about what is going on at the other side of the table. Although it is in your best interest to earn more money for yourself, it is likely in the best interest of the hiring company to save money and not pay you any more than they have to. In other words, it is unlikely the organization will do you a favor and pay you more without being asked.

4. *Value comes in different forms.* The idea of value here is a critical piece of the job negotiation puzzle. It may be that you are not able to negotiate the salary you want, but the job has value nevertheless, either because you love the work, or it is a stepping-stone to something even better, like a higher-level job, a graduate program, or an important experience of another kind.

How to Get Paid What You Are Worth

1. Learn about the gender wage gap.
2. Learn how to negotiate effectively.
3. Get in the habit of recognizing and articulating your value.

CHAPTER FOUR

Budgeting and Saving: Needs versus Wants

Introduction

Budgeting and saving. They may seem like some of the less sexy financial topics, but believe it or not, they are definitely some of the most important, and most empowering!

Budgeting, in a way, is at the root of all financial management. Without a budget, it's hard to know how much you need to earn, how much you can spend, and how much you want to or need to save, and invest. Saving speaks for itself—it provides a pool of money that is accessible in the future for things we all need or may want. Budgeting and saving together can be powerful tools of financial independence.

Budgeting and saving encourage some pretty amazing money behaviors:

- Being intentional with money
- Distinguishing between needs and wants
- Articulating savings goals
- Having a spending plan for a set period of time
- Achieving financial security!

So in other words, they are tools for *empowerment*. The engagement of these money behaviors means budgeting and saving are the basis for financial planning, health, and security. And how can you help your teenager put down her financial roots and start down the path of financial security? Teaching her how to use budgeting as a tool of financial management, and saving as a tool to build wealth, is a great way to start.

A budget is a blueprint for spending and provides the foundation for managing money in a way that creates wealth through controlling spending and creating savings. Budgeting and saving require being intentional with money, meaning, having a plan and being conscious of where your money is going. Given that money can be emotional and mean a lot of different things to people—happiness, anxiety, self-worth, pain, among other things—it can be a challenge to be intentional with money. But knowing where your money is going, and where you want it to go in the future, is critical to building wealth. Budgeting and saving provide the means to be intentional with money.

Another boon to learning about the purportedly "unsexy" tools of budgeting and saving involves a fantastic set of related behaviors and principles. Just as income is a critical piece (as we learned in Chapter 3) to financial well-being, so is spending. And spending is one of the many places where money and society reach a nexus that is negative for girls and young women. Society pressures girls and women to conform and fit in to a specific kind of image, and to keep up with the latest trends, no matter what the cost. With everything from the right clothes and accessories, to body work and salon treatments, girls and young women these days can feel pressured to spend money to feel attractive and be "in style."

Sometimes this spending pressure can mean spending money you don't have. The peril of spending more than is earned is an important lesson when it comes to saving, but it also lays the groundwork for understanding the key economic concept of opportunity costs and debt. Due to the inarguable fact of opportunity costs—meaning, you can only spend money on one thing at a time—money spent on the "right" pair of shoes is money that cannot be saved, invested, or used to create wealth in any way. Spending money you don't have—on shoes or anything else—means incurring debt, which usually comes with an interest cost.

The basis of this analysis of what you have to have now, and what you want to save for in the future, is needs and wants, and goal setting. The needs versus wants analysis is an effective tool for all ages, from a preschooler to a senior citizen. It goes hand and hand with being intentional with money. For example, understanding that food is a "need," but going out to nice restaurants is a "want," provides a structure for understanding when money has to be spent and when it is a choice.

Goal setting is also an incredibly powerful tool in both financial management and in life. Goal setting is a brilliant psychological tool that helps provide ballast for delayed gratification. Especially for girls and younger women who lack prefrontal cortex development as a part of their life phase, having a structure, and an incentive, to put off spending to build saving is extremely helpful. Goal setting has also been shown to be an effective way to help create something special or get through adversity, including putting money aside for the future and not spending it on something wanted now.

Finally—and this is a scary and critical piece—is that women's savings rates can be precariously low, sometimes resulting in financial crisis at the end of life.[1] This form of financial insecurity is something that can be changed, with the right knowledge and behaviors, starting at a young age.

So let's get started!

Financial Nutrition® Method: Value and Opportunity

- Money as commodity
- Risk
- *Value*
- *Opportunity costs*
- Information

As we learned in Chapter 3, value can be monetary or psychic or many other things. We are going to look at this concept further, as well as the concept of opportunity costs in the context of budgeting and saving. Savings goals foster more intentional spending, meaning, they provide a framework to prevent losing an opportunity to buy something important down the road by spending it on less-important things in the short term.

The concept of *value* can be explored and understood in many ways, but the needs versus wants analysis that goes along with budgeting and saving is a great way to understand value. Value is intimately related to whether something is a need or a want and how much spending—if any at all—should be committed to something.

Opportunity costs is another critical concept that comes up very plainly and clearly in the budgeting and saving analysis. An opportunity cost is the cost of a choice not taken, and the cost can mean a lot of things. In the financial sense, a cost could be the potential to make or earn more money, by spending the money on something else. So, for example, if you spend all of your money rather than save it or invest it, you may be losing an opportunity to build wealth and financial security.

Budgeting, Saving, and . . . Books?!!

When I work with young women in high school and college, I frequently ask questions to gauge their financial experience and acumen. One of the first questions I ask is about tracking spending, and budgeting, to see if my students have had any experience with that basic yet critical form of financial management.

I typically get an array of responses, as varied as if and how they receive money from parents, work, or gifts. Mostly, though, budgeting is not a familiar skill to them. In fact, when we do a budgeting exercise, it is clear that the students have very little experience with knowing and understanding what things cost and how to plan for different types of expenditures. Tracking spending is also not common among teenagers. Most of the girls I have taught manage their cash flow by spending their money and then not spending anything when they run out of money.

Experiential learning—or learning by doing—as we have discussed, can be a valuable tool for learning about money and financial management. The students in my classes do a really enlightening budget activity, where they complete budgets with two different levels of income but the same categories of necessary expenditures. The categories include real-life, adult-spending categories like housing, food, transportation, clothing, and loan payments. In the first column, the students get essentially an unlimited income and can then put any number in the spending categories, with the goal to address the kind of lifestyle they hope to have one day. In the second column, they have a monthly income number that is more representative of what they would earn in an early job after college, and includes paying taxes.

Needless to say, the two columns can look pretty different! But the realization the girls get is that there are many different lifestyles and ways to live and spend money. And there is a clear instructional narrative in the budgeting process, once the students have had a chance to design a life with everything they *want*, to then more carefully design a life with everything they *need*. They learn how to prioritize, and get creative—they come up with ideas like walking to work, instead of driving or taking public transportation; finding free fun activities instead of expensive entertainment options; living with friends instead of in their own, private, luxurious home. The budget exercise is meaningful and fruitful because it teaches both a life skill—budgeting—and a mindset—financially prioritizing needs versus wants.

When I talk to my students about saving and whether or not the girls save their money, and how, I again get a full range of responses. Many of my students do not save, mostly because they do not need to as their financial needs are covered. The material expectations for this age group are much higher than in previous generations. Many of them have iPhones, no matter the income level, and they did not have to save for them. Frequently, if the students have or make money, it is spent right away on the increasing, high-priced, "needs" of teenagers today.

For those students who do save, I ask about the mechanism for saving. Some of them have "formal" savings accounts in banks. They do not have much of an understanding of how interest works or the point of compound interest, but it seems like having the money somewhere inaccessible helps with saving.

More often than not, the young women who save money have more "informal" mechanisms, some of which may have the primary goal of keeping the money hidden from younger brothers and sisters! My students keep their saved money in their room, in drawers, or maybe under the mattress. Again, there seems to be little understanding of money as a commodity that can earn more money, or even about how to keep track of it and grow it in other ways.

My favorite story of saving—and I have actually heard it now from two different students—is the book savings plan. The idea is to stick money into different books, inserting a $10 or $20 bill, when it's received, between the pages of a book, and then putting the book back on the shelf. No record is kept of which money is in which book or even how much is saved. In fact, frequently the money is forgotten about, only to be discovered unexpected—and happily—when one of the "savings books" is read again.

So what are the benefits to this unconventional savings method? The pros: The saved money stays hidden from siblings and from the hider. Out of sight, out of mind—so it does not get spent. The cons: The bills stay so hidden that the saver cannot remember where they are! Nor do they have any record of how much money they are actually saving. Although the money is happily discovered from time to time, it can be a less effective savings plan as some of the money is never recovered.

The needs versus wants concept is an easier one to understand, even if it is not thoroughly being exercised. In my classes, we do a simple exercise where we make a list of needs and then a list of wants. What becomes evident immediately as the lists take shape on the board, side by side, is the overlap—or spectrum—of items on the needs and the wants lists.

The girls understand the trickiest part of this analysis—that within categories of absolute needs like food and shelter, there is a range of possibility, and that range includes everything from very basic needs to extremely improbable wants. For example, although food is a need, buying luxury food items like sushi or going out to fancy, expensive restaurants are both wants. Similarly, sharing a reasonably priced apartment with a group of friends is one form of housing, and living in a palace is another.

One great result of the needs versus wants analysis is that it strikes at the heart of peer pressure and societal ideas around spending money. There is cultural pressure that can make a "want" feel like a "need." Societal pressure means that there are things that we "have" to have, when in reality we might not even need them. Being able to do an objective needs versus wants analysis can help girls understand what they really need to have for a healthy life and not what they think they have based on the dictates of friends, social media, television shows, or movies.

Women Are Saving Less, at Great Cost

Saving is important for so many reasons. But one of the most important reasons to save throughout a lifetime is for that time, in old age, when it is no longer possible to work and earn income. It can be hard to imagine that time, and maybe even painful to think about, because it may be a time in life people aren't looking forward to.

Much has been published and discussed about regarding the gender wage gap and the challenges women face with money. Although there is great concern about all these issues, one dangerous trend that is not discussed as frequently is the financial crisis point women can reach in retirement. Women are almost twice as likely than men to live below the poverty line in retirement.[2] Lower savings throughout life, ending in poverty at the end of life, can be a culmination of the multitude of issues women deal with around money.

Saving for retirement can be a bigger issue for women than for men, for a variety of reasons. Although some studies show that women are better savers than men, they typically earn less.[3] Some data show that on average, women earn far less than what men do over a lifetime, and consequently, men have average retirement account balances that are 50 percent higher than women's.[4] And if you earn less, chances are you are going to save less.

Here are some of the key factors that combine to lead to potential end-of-life saving crises for women:

- *Earning less.* Women earn about 78 cents on the dollar compared to men, according to the U.S. Department of Labor.[5]
- *Working less.* Women have 12 years less in the paid workforce, according to the AARP Public Policy Institute.[6]

- *Living longer.* Women have a higher life expectancy than men, according to the Social Security Administration.[7]

The bottom line is that women earn less over a lifetime and live longer than men. Saving, and investing (which we will cover in Chapter 7), become critical needs for women and something important to teach to girls. But how can women save sufficiently for retirement, with all of these financial and life trends stacked against them? One financial dynamic that can help is saving early, because of the power of compounding. Starting to save early in life can be vital for women, so compounding can really work its magic over a life that may perhaps include less income and more years.

When I work with teenagers and we talk about saving for retirement, I understand that it is hard for them to think about a time when they will be too old and infirmed to work. In fact, some of them are not even able to envision a time when they will have to work to support themselves at all! Which in turn means it can be hard for them to feel the urgency of negotiating well for their first job out of college, and every other job thereafter, and starting to save and invest as early as possible.

So I show in class a great example of how powerful it is to start saving early—through the power of compounding—that literally leaves my students speechless. In Chapter 5, we will get into the real nitty-gritty of compounding, including the math behind it, but this example shows the power of saving early, without showing the magic that goes on behind the compounding curtain, yet.

In my classes, we look at a chart that compares two hypothetical friends with different saving patterns. Friend 1 invests savings of $2,000 per year from age 19 to age 26 (a total of $16,000 invested) and then keeps the money invested until she is 65. Throughout the ages of 19–65, the investment is earning a return of 12 percent. Friend 2 invests savings of $2,000 per year from age 27 to 65 (a total of $78,000), earning a 12 percent return the entire time, as well. When I ask the students to guess who has more money in the end, inevitably they guess Friend 2, who has a base investment of $62,000 more—or more than four times as much—than Friend 1.

But lo and behold, due to the power of Friend 1 starting to save earlier than Friend 2 (again, more about this fantastic financial dynamic in Chapter 5), Friend 1 is actually over $750,000 ahead of Friend 2 in the end, despite the much smaller initial investment. The reason is because Friend 1 started investing eight years earlier. The beauty of this exercise beyond the obvious power of compound interest is that it shows that people with less money can still save extremely productively over a long period of time, if they start young. Although a return of 12 percent per year is higher than typical, compound interest is powerful with lower rates of return as well.

The story paints a compelling picture for saving early and also presents a strong argument for educating girls about money. The power of saving early can have a huge impact on a financial life, including one that may otherwise be at a disadvantage. Given the power of early savings, and its ability to make even smaller amounts grow large over time, educating girls to understand and use saving early in their lives to their advantage early on is key to helping them grow up to live a financially healthy life.

Opportunity Analysis

It's clear that saving is important for women and that budgeting can be a great tool to get there. But saving can be tricky, and potentially undesirable, even with tools like budgeting. It all goes back to the behavioral component of money—even if we know what's right, we don't always do it. We may want to spend all of the money we have, and possibly even more, on something right away. We don't want to forgo having something we want or something that someone else has. That is a very powerful impulse for people of all ages. So, part of changing behavior, is changing disposition, and that can come from a deeper understanding of economic incentives and how money works.

Having goals, and understanding opportunity costs with money, are two great ways to change both disposition and behavior. When it comes to following a budget, and forgoing immediate wants and desires to save money for a time in our life we may not even be able to imagine, we need all the help we can get!

Let's start with the idea of savings goals. Goals are a proven motivator in many areas of life—athletics, careers, and not least of all, money. Among other things, goals provide an incentive, and an intentional option, when giving in to something immediate is easier, more fun, or less painful. You get the picture—goals provide fortification and a happy reason to delay gratification. Having goals means something positive to look forward to in the future, something to work toward, something to measure steps toward and achieve mini-successes along the way. Goals can help enormously with saving—knowing the future holds a trip to Europe, a new car or house, or a child's college education makes it that much easier to cook at home instead of going out for dinner, or buy the less expensive outfit.

The economic issue of opportunity costs is a really important one to understand as well, and it plays right into having goals. An opportunity cost is the cost of alternatives not chosen, as money can only be spent on one thing at a time. For example, the opportunity cost of spending a lot of money on cheeseburgers might be not having that money to put toward a gym membership, or a trip to the Bahamas, or a stock fund. Savings goals foster more intentional spending, meaning, they provide a framework to prevent losing an opportunity to buy something important down the road by spending it on less important things in the short term.

In other words, money can only be spent in one place at one time. Understanding the cost of something you are not getting can be every bit as valuable as understanding the cost of something you are getting. It is a fuller and more complete analysis. Coupled with goals, opportunity costs come to life and help fill in the missing pieces of the puzzle of how money can help achieve the life we want.

We don't always have a choice of when we need to spend money. But it is a great thing to understand opportunity costs at a young age when the stakes are a little lower. For adult women, an opportunity cost might involve losing out on owning a home or saving enough for retirement. Young women who learn this concept as teenagers will be one step ahead in financial know-how and as adults will better understand how to seize opportunities to their economic advantage.

The Power of an Allowance

Teaching kids about money can be a serious challenge for families. One of the most common problems I hear from parents is that it is difficult to teach something so abstract. Meaning, because kids do not take out mortgages and credit cards, they do not have the actual experience of taking financial responsibility, going through a challenging financial process, and learning from their financial mistakes and failures.

When I introduce the topic of money management in classes I teach to teenagers, I ask if any of the students receive an allowance. Only about one-third of the class usually raises their hands. Many teenagers seem to receive money on demand, meaning, if they need something they ask for the money and then get it, or not. They may have access to credit cards or debit cards, so they never even handle money.

Giving teenagers an allowance in cash can help teach them real money management. My students always tell me that having real cash makes them think about money very differently than having a credit card or debit card at their disposal. If they are going to use a credit or debit card, they need to have access to a record of what they are spending, so that spending feels real in the same way that disappearing cash does. In addition, young people should write down what they spend money on for a full month, until they have a clear sense of their spending dynamic and where their money is going.

Receiving a weekly allowance, along with some guidance on how to start their money management, provides an amazing opportunity for hands-on financial management. Having an allowance provides a girl with an opportunity to practice money management at a young age. And with some help and guidance, she will be setting a foundation for the much more complicated—and vital—financial management required of an adult.

Simply put, the beauty of an allowance is it provides kids with that all-important *experiential* aspect of money. This means that kids actually get to handle money: spend it, save it, plan for how to use it, and even run out of it sometimes. The great thing about the younger set practicing with money with support and guidance is that they are practicing, succeeding, and sometimes failing at financial management before the stakes are too high.

Do Try This at Home!

Goal setting with money is such an important tool that we wanted to provide an activity around it to try at home. Feel free to try it with your teenager!

1. Set a savings goal, along with a time period to reach the goal.
2. Write down how much you will need to save each week to achieve your goal.
3. For each savings week, determine your income and how much you can spend (or not) to reach your weekly savings goal.

For a teenager, income might include allowance, earnings from part-time jobs, or gifts. But just like adults, it's possible that teenagers have to, or choose to, spend more money than they earn in a week.

Spending some time away from home for the summer can be an opportunity for teens to manage money on their own for the first time. Because money learning is so experiential, this opportunity can be a first step for a young person to learn to manage money effectively—and independently.

If your child is going to camp, to a program on a university campus or overseas, or has a job for the first time, here are some ideas to get started on money management at a young age.

1. *Budget.* Creating a spending plan is an excellent first step. For a camp or program away from home, establish how much money your young person will have to spend for the period of the program. For a job, the teen can project

out expected income for the summer. Then, put together a budget that includes money to be spent per day, week, or month on different items like food, clothes, transportation, and souvenirs. For income earners, a category in the budget for savings is also a great idea.

2. *Accounting.* Before the program or job starts, work with your teen to develop an accounting system that fits their lifestyle best. This may be a small notebook that can be carried around in a pocket or a backpack, or maybe a budgeting app for a smartphone. The idea is to keep track of daily expenditures and add them up each day to determine if spending is on track per the predefined budget.

3. *Practice.* It is always a good idea to practice this method for 2–3 weeks before the child leaves home. That way, any problems can be worked out of the system, adjustments made, and questions answered.

This money management system can be a strong precursor to college accounting as well. If your teen tries this system for a couple of summers before leaving for college, independent financial management in college will be much easier. Spending time away from home in the summer is a great opportunity for personal development. Money management skills can be a part of that development too.

Discussion Points

Here are some additional discussion points you can share with the young woman in your life about how to budget and save, to create wealth and meet goals in her life. Financial conversations using these discussion points can be had whenever is convenient—at breakfast, in the car, during family time, or a specially prescribed time to talk about money in a group or a club.

1. *The importance of goal setting.* Goals are important in any area of your life, because they allow you to dream and to become the best person you can be. You can have goals with school, sports, or artistic endeavors, among other things. Goals are important with money because they help you understand things you might want or need in the future, so you can put money aside to make sure you have those things. It is tempting to buy everything you want today, but there may be bigger things you can afford by saving that you can focus on and make a plan for, so that you don't spend today, and save for the future.

2. *What is the difference between needs and wants?* It is a great thing to know what you *need* to have versus what you *want* to have. In some ways it is obvious what you need—things like food and clothes—and obvious what you just might want—things like concert tickets or video games. The tricky thing, though, is that needs and wants often overlap or exist together on a spectrum. For example, you need food and

you need clothes. The "want" part of the analysis comes in when you look at the range of food and clothes. For example, you could go out to eat at a fancy restaurant, or you could buy food at the grocery store and cook it yourself. So the needs and wants analysis applies both across categories of things, and within them too. You could buy the hot designer clothes that everyone wants, or you can buy clothes on sale. Understanding the difference between needs and wants can also help you deal with the marketing pressures that you *have* to have what everyone else has, and really focus your money on things that are meaningful to you.

3. *Know your spending habits.* It can be a challenge to be conscious with money, so an important step in managing your money is to understand where it is going. Sometimes we spend money without realizing it, or knowing just what things cost. Money also has an emotional component, meaning it can make us feel happy, sad, anxious, successful, or entitled. By keeping track of your money, you can be more intentional about the way you spend it and not get lost in the emotions that might come with it. Even more important, you will know exactly where it is going, so you can direct it more carefully if you have savings goals, or want to start spending money more carefully based on your analysis of what you need versus what you want.

4. *Think about a spending plan.* A spending plan, or a budget, is a great way to manage your money so you have what you need now and for the future. A budget is a tool that can help you figure out how to spend less than you earn and how to make sure you have the money for the things you need. It is a tool you can use throughout your life.

How to Budget and Save Effectively

1. Set a savings goal for something you would like to have in the future.
2. Determine the needs versus wants in your spending patterns.
3. Create and follow a budget that allows you to save by spending less than you earn.

CHAPTER FIVE

Compound Interest: You Can Understand This!

Introduction

Compound interest is one of the most basic—and most powerful—forces in the world of money. The concept of interest, in general, also clarifies the real purpose of money as a commodity and a means to achieve the life we want. So interest is a great concept to learn early and apply throughout life.

As we have discussed, money means a lot of different things to people. It can be emotional and anxiety or joy provoking. It can represent success, happiness, status, greed, or misery. When I teach about money, one concept I really want my students to understand is that at the simplest level of all, money is a commodity, not something magical or mystical. Money is a tool, a means, to help create the life that you want. This idea helps make money management more objective and less emotional. And it also makes clear that the power is in the hands of the manager of the money—*we* make the decisions of how we want to manage our money, not the other way around.

What is a commodity, exactly? Dictionary.com defines a commodity as:

1. an article of trade or commerce, especially a product as distinguished from a service.
2. something of use, advantage, or value.[1]

Understanding the idea that money is a commodity clarifies the fact that money is a tool and really puts money in its place. Money is a tool to take care of yourself financially, and understanding how to use it effectively is what financial literacy is all about. So if money is a tool, a means of exchange to get what we need and want, then money has value. And like anything of value, money has a cost.

The cost of money is known as "interest." Interest is owed when someone else's money is used (in the case of borrowing money as with a consumer loan), and interest is earned when our money is being used by someone else (as in the case of lending it or putting it in a bank). If we don't have the money, we can't use it to earn income through investing, or buy things that have value for us, so we want to get paid for not having the use of the money. The same concepts apply when we borrow money.

The idea that money has a cost is a foundational concept in finance. It underlies critical financial concepts like compound interest, which is in turn related to important consumer products like credit cards and investments. Understanding the power of compound interest and using it as an advantage can help a consumer avoid credit card debt and help an investor build wealth through investing over long periods of time.

The relationship between interest and risk is also a key foundational concept in finance, as it is the basis for how much you will have to spend if you borrow money, and how much you may get paid if you lend, or invest it. In short, if you are considered a risky borrower in that it is unlikely you will pay back money that you borrow in full, or by the terms that you originally agreed to, you will have to pay a higher interest rate, and that loan will cost you more money. By the same token, if you invest in an asset that is considered risky, or less likely to pay a good return, when you do get paid it may be a higher value.

Another important aspect to understand about interest rates in a larger, macroeconomic sense, is that they fluctuate in ways beyond our control. Base interest rates in general depend on national and global conditions, and that in turn can impact the individual. Base interest rate levels are macroeconomic, and the consumer's interest for loans like cars, homes, and credit cards will fluctuate along with the country's interest rates that are set by the government.

And what happens on a global or national scale can impact each one of us individually. When it comes to financial dynamics, interest rates are a perfect example of how global or national economic conditions can affect an individual's financial situation. When interest rates increase at the global or national level, it means that interest rates will increase for the consumer, making borrowing more expensive. This dynamic can apply to car loans, or home loans, or credit card rates, or any kind of consumer loan. And when borrowing gets more expensive, it costs money, and can add stress to personal finances.

Financial Nutrition® Method: Costs, Risks, Costs!

- *Money as commodity*
- *Risk*
- Value
- Opportunity costs
- Information

Interest is the cost of money, plain and simple. It is a clear dynamic of money that shows that it is a *commodity*—it has a cost, like anything else. The cost of money varies with risk, both when you're borrowing money and when you're earning money as an investor. But the beauty of the concept of money as a commodity is that money becomes a tool, plain and simple, not something magical, mystical, and impossible to control or understand. Money becomes a means to achieving the life you want to have, and that is a form of empowerment like no other.

Interest rates in general also begin to develop that extremely important financial concept of *risk*. Risk is the chance that something will go badly, and it applies in many ways in finance. If money is lent, there is the chance it will not be paid back. If money is invested, there is the chance that money will be lost. Interest rates tend to fluctuate with risk, meaning, the more likely the borrower is to be unreliable in paying money back, the higher interest rate that borrower will have to pay.

Compounding, Einstein, and Math

Compounding is where it's at! Seriously. Compound interest is a key factor in borrowing, saving, and investing. But few people understand its incredible power or how it works, except maybe Albert Einstein. Yes, *the* Albert Einstein. According to Einstein, "Compound interest is the eighth wonder of the world. [S]He who understands it, earns it . . . [s]he who doesn't . . . pays it."[2]

One of the contributing factors to the power of compound interest is the math behind the formula. For some inexplicable reason, girls think they are not good at math. So, here we have a math-based concept that is hard for just about everyone to get except Einstein, which means given the math phobia, it could potentially be even harder for girls. But we *all* have to get it, because it is a key financial principle and a huge contributor to building wealth.

When I teach girls about compound interest, I always start with the concept of simple interest. The funny thing about simple interest and money is that consumers are rarely charged simple interest for the money they borrow. Instead, borrowers are charged compound interest, which is basically an exponential version of simple interest, which is why it is so powerful and can add up so quickly, at significant cost to the borrower.

When I bring up simple interest in my classes, my students get a slightly familiar look in their eyes and tend to say something like, "Didn't we learn that in middle school?" But not much more than that is remembered. Simple interest—like any mathematical formula—usually gets taught in math class. Although math is of critical importance and done way more commonly in everyday matters than many of us realize, sometimes it does not "stick" unless integrated into a more practical expression. The other issue about simple interest is, unless it is used as a conceptual stepping stone for compound interest, it is not typically a rate you will pay on a multiyear loan.

Now it's time to understand how interest is calculated. Let's first take a look at the simple interest formula, and enjoy its simplicity. Simple interest is calculated as:

$$I = P * R * T$$

or

$$I(nterest) = P(rincipal) * R(ate) * T(ime)$$

For example, to know the amount of interest you would have to pay on the principal of a loan of $1,000, at 10 percent interest, for four years, the equation would look like:

$$I(nterest) = \$1,000 \text{ (Principal)} * .10 \text{ (Rate)} * 4 \text{ (Time)}$$

so

$$I(nterest) = \$1,000 * .10 * 4$$

or

$$I(nterest) = \$400$$

Table 5.1   Simple Interest

	Principal	Annual Simple Interest Owed	Total Simple Interest Owed (or Earned)	Total Owed (or Earned)
Year 1	$1,000	$100	$100	$1,100
Year 2	$1,000	$100	$200	$1,200
Year 3	$1,000	$100	$300	$1,300
Year 4	$1,000	$100	$400	$1,400

In other words, 10 percent of $1,000 is $100, so the interest paid is $100 per year, or $400 for four years in total.

The beauty of simple interest from the perspective of the borrower is that the only interest that is paid is on the principal, or the original amount of the loan. So if the loan is held for four years with interest accruing the whole time, the interest paid on the loan is one year of interest, times four years. This is true even if the interest is not paid each year, but is carried over into the next year and accumulates to increase the size of the original amount owed. So, for example, Table 5.1 shows what the interest payment picture would look like.

Simple, right?

Let's complicate things a little now, to begin to crack the all-important concept—and dynamic—of compound interest. What would happen if you had to pay interest on the interest you owed, that accumulates over a period of time? Would that be more or less money than simple interest? It's not exactly so simple, anymore, when you start talking about paying interest on interest. But it can—and must—be learned.

Let's start by looking at the first scenario a little differently. Some of the elements will stay the same—a loan of $1000 (the principal), borrowed for four years, at an interest rate of 10 percent. But this time, rather than just paying interest on the principal this year, interest will be paid on both the principal, and the interest that has accrued each year. Table 5.2 shows this scenario.

In the second case, each year you pay interest on the principal ($1,000), as well as the interest for that year. Although in the simple interest example the interest cost each year stays the same, in the compound interest example the interest cost rises steadily each year. The best way to see the difference is to compare the final repayment amount after Year 4:

Simple interest example: $1,400

Compound interest example: $1,464

Difference: $64 or 16 percent more interest paid ($400 compared to $464)

Table 5.2   Compound Interest

	Principal	Interest	Total Compound Interest Owed (or Earned)	Total Owed (or Earned)
Year 1	$1,000	$100	$100	$1,100
Year 2	$1,000	$110	$210	$1,210
Year 3	$1,000	$121	$331	$1,331
Year 4	$1,000	$133	$464	$1,464

So what happened? The interest charge in the compound interest scenario increases exponentially. In this case, the interest was compounded annually, meaning, once a year interest was charged on whatever was owed up until that point. In actuality, interest can be compounded over all sorts of periods as well, like daily or monthly, as well as annually. The more frequently interest is compounded, the faster it grows.

Here is the formula for compound interest:

$$I(nterest) = P(rincipal) * [(1 + R(ate))^{t(ime)} - 1]$$

Compare this to the simple interest formula:

$$I = P(rincipal) * R(ate) * T(ime)$$

One of the key differences is that the T(ime) factor increases the interest exponentially. Exponential in this case has two meanings: both a mathematical exponent and an accelerating rate.

Another way to understand compounding is with a handy concept called the "Rule of 72." The Rule of 72 is a way to figure out the number of years it will take to double your money (either that you would earn through an investment or that you owe if you borrowed money). The way the equation works is this:

Years required to double *investment* (or *amount owed*) = 72 ÷ compound interest

Although the examples and scenarios above not only show how compound interest works and why it is so powerful, they also show how important math can be in understanding money. In fact, studies show that there is a correlation between understanding math and being financially literate. We just did the math for one of the most critical and foundational concepts in finance—compound interest—and it was not that compli-cated or difficult to reason out. In many cases, it's enough to understand the formula and the underlying forces and properties. Calculators are suf-ficient for doing the math in high finance, especially as the numbers get larger and the scenarios get more complicated.

Math, Math, Math

Speaking of math, it is clear at this point that finance has a basis in math, and a person's comfort and facility with math can help with a deeper understanding of financial concepts and behaviors.[3] Math comes into play with financial understanding in different ways and at different levels. First, there is the big-picture understanding of money—knowing that it is impor-tant to budget, save for the future, manage debt and taxes, have insurance just in case. Then there is the equally important action of doing the neces-sary calculations for budgeting, projecting future needs for income, saving, paying taxes, figuring out how much insurance might be needed.

The math in financial management can get more complicated than that, however. Quantifying risk, comparing interest rates, knowing if a monthly mortgage payment is affordable, understanding the power and meaning of compound interest, means that being able to understand the math behind the concepts is critical. Of course, calculators and experts exist to help with more complicated equations, but it is useful to understand the underlying mathematical concepts of all different types of finance.

However, a myth exists that girls are not good at math, and that myth is very destructive when it comes to financial empowerment in women. Girls and math have been a subject under scrutiny for some time. Although many people may not feel comfortable with math or the STEM (science, technology, engineering, math) fields in general, the female gender seems to be lagging particularly in these areas. Some estimates show that the number of women in the STEM fields is as low as 24 percent, while women now make up about half of the overall work force.[4]

Studies show that financial literacy and math understanding may be linked.[5] So this poses an additional challenge to girls who feel undercon-fident in math. In fact, if financial literacy and math are inextricably linked, girls are particularly at risk with engaging around finance if they are falling behind in math.

Carol Dweck at Stanford University did an excellent, eye-opening study about girls and math. The study, entitled "Is Math a Gift? Beliefs That Put Females at Risk," shows that viewing math ability as a gift can make young women more susceptible to a loss of confidence and lower performance in math when faced with difficulty and stereotyping. But more importantly, the study showed that sending a message that these abilities can be developed can do away with that vulnerability to lower math confidence.[6] Given the statistics about STEM-related fields and lack of adult women role models in these areas—and in the financial industry—it is clear that girls may well imagine that their gender does not have what it takes to do math or succeed in math-related fields.

When I teach girls and young women about money and finance, I find that they understand the material easily, are interested, engaged, and empowered. But the teacher and approach are an important part of any kind of effective education. Girls, math, and the STEM fields may be another case of where society is sending a message that girls are receiving and accepting. If girls themselves think that girls are bad at math, they might believe that they are. If there are few women role models in the STEM fields, it sends a message to girls that women can't do those jobs.

The financial industry bemoans the lack of women's engagement around money, but studies and anecdotal evidence show that women do not appreciate the way that the industry currently talks to them, or teaches them, about money. As such, the industry is attempting to try to market to women more effectively, with an awareness of women's growing economic power in the United States.

The ability to understand math—and finance—for girls and young women is not based on an inherent talent or gift. Girls and young women can be engaged around money and math in an environment where the educators believe in their ability. The current culture around financial understanding seems to be that being effective with money is only a possibility for a select, lucky few. With the right education and awareness, we can debunk that myth and help our girls develop the confidence around money, finance, and math that they need to be financially successful.

Where Do Interest Rates Come From?

Let's go back to the idea of interest rates and what they really mean. It is clear that money has a cost and that cost is called interest. Compounding is a powerful force and also a key element in credit, debt, saving, and investing. The cost of money also comes into play in more complicated financial topics like rate of return, which is a calculation of earnings from an investment. The cost of money is also a factor in the concept of the time value of money, which is a dynamic that involves the potential earning rate of money, meaning that money received sooner has more value because of its earning potential.

Although some of these ideas, like rate of return and time value of money, seem like concepts that would only be grappled with in a business school classroom or in the conference rooms of high finance, the reality is all of these elements of the idea of money having a cost are critical to decision making about how to use money. These decisions could be simple like whether to make a purchase, or more complicated, like whether to borrow a lot of money or to put money into investments. It is easy to see as well how the cost of money factors in to financial behaviors like budgeting.

Let's go a step further and talk about how that cost, or interest rate, gets determined, because the cost of money—whether you are paying it as a borrower or being paid it as a saver or investor—can have a huge impact on your financial health, wealth, and well-being.

Interest rates that are specific to financial products like car loans, mortgages, credit cards, and other kinds of consumer loans are based on the borrower's perceived risk. Risk means simply the possibility that something bad will happen. When it comes to borrowing, lending, and investing money, the risk is that you won't get your money back or you won't earn much return on your investment. We'll discuss the specifics of consumer risk analysis in Chapter 6.

But for now, it's helpful to understand that the relationship between interest and risk is a critical foundational concept in finance, as it is the basis for how much you will have to spend if you borrow money, and how much you may get paid if you lend, or invest it. In short, if you are considered a risky borrower in that it is unlikely you will pay back money that you borrow in full, or by the terms that you originally agreed to, you will have to pay a higher interest rate, and that loan will cost you more money. By the same token, if you invest in an asset that is considered risky, or less likely to pay a good return, when you do get paid it may be a higher value. We'll be looking at the cost and benefit of risk more thoroughly in both Chapter 6 on debt and credit and in Chapter 7 on investing.

But there is a rate at which banks, and other primary lenders, borrow from each other, and that rate is set by the government. This rate, in turn, impacts the interest rates consumers have to pay, because lenders will charge more to loan money to consumers than they are paying to borrow from each other or the government.

Interestingly, the macroeconomic basis for interest rates means that economic forces on a national and international level play a role in determining interest rates. Those rates are typically related to the current level of economic growth and inflation in the United States, which in turn can be impacted by both local and national factors. The U.S. government, specifically the Federal Reserve Board, determines the base rate of lending in the United States as a form of monetary policy, or policy to help the economy and the consumer stay financially healthy and robust.

The idea is that if interest rates are lower, then money is "cheaper," so both consumers and corporations will borrow more money. When spent and put into the economy, this borrowed money will help make the economy stronger, because the money pays for goods and services that get produced. The production of goods and services are the basis of the economy, and also mean that people are earning money participating in those industries. But if the economy becomes too strong and people are spending a lot, inflation may increase, which is considered mostly a negative economic force as it decreases the purchasing power of the consumer by making things more expensive.

When the economy heats up and produces higher inflation, the government may raise base interest rates so that money becomes more "expensive." The banks and other lenders borrow from each other and the government at a higher rate, and they pass that cost along to consumers. When money becomes more expensive, both consumers and corporations tend to borrow less, which helps slow the economy down as spending and production decrease.

Interest in Interest Rates?

As you can see, interest rates are a very important concept for young people to understand, as they really do connect critical areas of finance and economics—the cost of money, risk, and macroeconomics. Compounding also addresses the key ways to make money with saving and investing, and how quickly debt can grow when money is owed. But for young women, one of the crucial dynamics of money that interest rates emphasize is the idea of money being a commodity.

When I work with young women in high school and college, it is clear that they are well aware of the struggles that they will face throughout life, especially if they want everything that life can offer—interesting work, earning potential, and family. And as we have discussed in this book, women already face an uphill battle when it comes to wealth building, because of many factors, including earning less and living longer than men. Additionally, some women may want a life where they can be both worker and mother, and that means somehow striking the proverbial "work-life balance," which can be a challenge given that a person can only ever be in one place at one time.

So in my classes, we talk about the need to understand money and the importance of having the skills to manage it. Issues like understanding income potential and negotiating salaries, and saving early are critical to understand to ensure adequate savings for retirement. Interestingly, the concept of compounding impacts both of those issues. Negotiating a high starting salary out of college can make a huge difference in overall income earned because salary increases are frequently percentage changes over the previous salary. In this way, salaries are compounded, so the higher level you start with at a younger age, the more the income can increase over time. This is the same idea with compounding with saving—saving at a younger age with more years to compound interest means a greater end result with less money having to be saved.

Additionally, as young women look into the future at their hopes, dreams, and possibilities, with all they plan to accomplish professionally, creatively, and personally, understanding that money is a way to help them get there—not the answer in the end—is key to helping them utilize money as a tool. It helps with that all-important disposition, which as we have discussed, can then result in changed behavior. The disposition, or mind-set, that money is a commodity, or means to an end, can mean a greater empowerment over understanding it and using it effectively.

Do Try This at Home!

Compound interest is powerful, as we all (including Albert Einstein!) agree. And the math behind it is important, of course. But research has shown that compound interest can be one of the hardest financial concepts for consumers to understand.[7] Although it's not clear why that challenge exists, it is a problem as compounding can help so much on the saving and investing side, and hurt so much financially on the borrowing and debt side.

But as with most things in finance, you don't have to go it alone when you are dealing with compounding. It's important to understand the formula, and the exponential dynamic of the increases over time, but you can also use special compounding calculators to help figure out just how much you will gain with saving or investing over time—or spend on interest when borrowing money.

The Internet provides lots of possibilities for online calculators. Try typing into your browser "compounding calculators," and pick a high-quality option, like one sponsored by the government. Now, play around with it a little. Have some fun—put in some saving and borrowing scenarios with the amount of money saved or borrowed, an interest rate anywhere between 5 and 15 percent, and a period of time ranging from 1 to 30 years. Try different scenarios like 1, 5, and 10 years, and see how much you will have gained by saving—or spent by borrowing, due to the power of compounding. See if you agree with Albert Einstein, that compounding is one of the most powerful forces in the universe!

Discussion Points

Here are some additional discussion points you can share with the young woman in your life about how interest works on a micro and macro level, and how to manage the cost of interest to her benefit. Financial conversations using these discussion points can be had whenever is convenient—at breakfast, in the car, during family time, or a specially prescribed time to talk about money in a group or a club.

1. *The cost of money.* When you use other people's money—when you borrow and when other people use your money—when you lend, save, or invest, money will have a cost, and that is known as interest. Money can be used to make more money, so it is not free. It is what is known as a "commodity," or something of use or value. Understanding how interest works can help you learn to both minimize the cost you pay for money and maximize the cost others pay you.
2. *The power of compounding.* Compound interest is a powerful force in the universe. When money is borrowed over a period of time and interest accumulates, compounding means that interest is not just being paid on the original loan, or principal, but it is also being paid on the interest. For this reason, the value of the interest over time can rise exponentially. There are different ways, like interest rate calculators and the Rule of 72, you can calculate compound interest. But either way, it is important to understand the math behind it and to know that everyone can do math!
3. *Risky business.* The cost of money is frequently directly connected to, or correlated with, risk. Risk is the potential that something bad will happen. In the world of money, or more specifically, lending and investing, risk is the potential that as a borrower you will not pay back the money you borrowed in full and/or on time. As an investor, risk is the potential that you will not earn the money you expect to earn, or perhaps lose your investment money altogether. Interest, or the cost of money, tends to move higher as perceived risk is greater. This means that you can pay more interest if you are a risky borrower, which costs you more money. At this same time, if you are investing in a risky investment, you have the potential to earn more money from it, although that is not guaranteed.
4. *The big picture.* The basis for the interest rates we pay or earn as consumers is macroeconomic, meaning economic forces on a national and international level. Those interest rates are usually related to economic

strength, and inflation, in the United States and the world. The U.S. government, specifically the Federal Reserve Board, sets the base interest rate from which all other interest rates grow, as a way to help the economy and the consumer stay healthy.

MANAGING THE COST OF MONEY

1. Learn the difference between compound interest and simple interest.
2. Learn how to calculate compound interest with an online interest calculator.
3. Think about how risk can impact the cost of money when you borrow, or what you might earn with an investment.

CHAPTER SIX

Debt and Credit: Let's Manage This

Introduction

I remember as a child thinking that credit cards were free money. I would watch my parents pay for things with a credit card, and I would think, I can't wait to get my hands on one of those so I can buy anything I want! I had no idea that a credit card was not free money—that anything purchased with the credit card would have to be repaid, and sometimes, repaid with interest. But that myth of credit cards as free money lived on in my mind through my teen years—to some consequence!

Sure enough, the first time I did get my hands on a credit card—with a fairly low credit limit, fortunately—it was the summer before my freshman year of college. I bought all kinds of things with the card and did not keep track of what I was spending, nor did I understand I needed to make payments to the card each month, with certain deadlines. Within a couple of months, I had maxed out the card without realizing anything about how to use it responsibly, pay it on time, or maybe even consider not using it at all!

Debt can be a friend indeed when one is in need. There may be times in a life when money needs to be borrowed for critical purchases. Such a thing exists, known as "good debt," which is debt that is used as a form of investment or debt that provides some sort of value, including coming at a fairly low interest rate. Examples of good debt are debt used to fund an education, if the expectation is that earning power can increase with the education. Another form of good debt is debt to used to buy a home, as the monthly payments go toward paying off the home and building equity, and house debt also has some tax benefits.

But there is also a downside to debt and the rapid accumulation of debt that can happen as a result of compound interest. Understanding when it makes sense to borrow money and how to manage debt responsibly are important. Young women need a strategy and to be intentional when borrowing money, and managing credit. One important concept regarding debt is credit history. Once a person takes out a loan—whether it is a credit card, a student loan, a car loan, or other types of loans—she impacts her credit history. A credit history is a listing, attached to a social security number, of all of the loans a person has, and the history of repayment, including whether the loans were repaid on time or not.

This means that every payment made or missed on a loan will be recorded with credit bureaus and included in that all-important financial metric, the credit score. The way credit is handled out of the gate can have a far-reaching impact on borrowing ability and interest rates. Credit is about trust, and lending institutions use credit scores as a mechanism to determine a borrower's likelihood to repay a loan, in other words, how financially trustworthy the borrower is.

It is also important to understand the different forms of debt that are available to consumers—everything from car loans to home loans to student loans. Along with understanding the types of debt are the logistics of the debt, including the way different kinds of loans are structured for repayment, and the different possible terms of the loans. Understanding and being responsible with these specific factors of debt will help in the process of maintaining a high credit score and a healthy credit history.

The interest rate paid on a loan is important, because it is a cost, and it takes money away from other things. Studies show that women paid higher interest rates on mortgages during the subprime mortgage crisis than they should have, given their credit score, which can be used as a gauge of creditworthiness. Because of opportunity costs, every penny you pay for a loan that you do not have to pay is a penny you cannot put somewhere else—an opportunity forgone. By the same token, the lower interest rates you get on a loan, the more loan you can afford. A lower rate on a mortgage could be the difference between being able to afford to own a home through borrowing with a mortgage, or renting.

Understanding the concept of the value of debt is also key in maintaining a healthy and powerful financial life—including analyzing whether the costs outweigh the financial benefits. Debt can be used as a form of investment, if the benefits of the debt are higher than the costs. This can be true in the case of financial investments, like borrowing money to buy a house. But it can also be true in the form of life investments. You can invest in yourself with education or professional development or other kinds of training, and that investment might yield greater income or increased happiness. In this case, the outcome may well be worth the cost of the debt.

Financial Nutrition® Method: Money, Risk, and Opportunity

- *Money as commodity*
- *Risk*
- Value
- *Opportunity costs*
- Information

Money in reality is a *commodity*, with a cost, as discussed in Chapter 5. When it comes to actually using credit and borrowing money, it is evident in a more practical way how money has a cost. The cost of money is known as interest, and interest, particularly compound interest, is a key element in credit, debt, saving, and investing. The reality of the idea of money having a cost is critical to decision making about how to use money. These decisions could be simple like whether to make a purchase, or more complicated, like whether to borrow a lot of money, or to put money into investments.

Risk is the possibility that something bad will happen, but it can also be costly. If you need to borrow money and are considered a risky borrower, your costs of borrowing will be higher. In this chapter, we will look at how that risk is measured in terms of the cost of money, which translates to interest rates and the cost of debt.

The cost of money is also related to a critical economic concept known as *opportunity cost*. Opportunity cost is a general term that can be applied to many things besides money. But in the case of money, an opportunity cost is the fact that the same money can only be spent on one thing at a time. So, money spent on a trip to Europe can not then be used as the down payment for a house. As opportunity costs are the costs of the alternatives not chosen, in this chapter we look at the cost of an opportunity taken— or not taken—when it involves borrowing money.

The Credit Horror Story!

I was fortunate that my parents were able to bail out my first unsuccessful attempt at using credit, learning a valuable lesson but keeping my early financial foundation stable, but not everyone is so lucky. In my classes for high school–aged girls, we watch a PBS video that I call "The Credit

Horror Story" about a young woman who goes off to college and promptly acquires—with the urging of many banks—a number of credit cards. The segment shows how the young woman is able to acquire a number of credit cards when she first comes to campus as a freshman and then racks up a huge amount of credit card debt in a short period of time.

In this situation, the young woman has to finance her living and college expenses on her own. Although she has a full-time job as a hostess at a local restaurant—working full-time along with going to college full-time—she still does not have enough money to pay for all of her expenses like books, food, and rent. In this state of financial desperation, and not fully understanding the ramifications of using credit cards, the young woman uses her array of new cards to help finance her life and educational expenses.

She quickly gets into trouble with her credit cards as she does not understand the need to pay the balances off, or a payment of any kind, by the deadline each month, or at all. In a fairly short amount of time, her credit card balances climb, because of the original charges, missed payments, late fees, and compound interest. When the young woman decides to address the issue, she has accumulated over $30,000 in credit card debt with no foreseeable way to pay it. She visits a credit counselor, who informs her that because her credit cards have been turned over to collection agencies, there is no way to negotiate with the credit card companies.

The Credit Horror Story has a big impact on my students, but I want to be sure the realization and understanding from the story has more than just shock value. So we talk about the type of credit the young woman in the story used to pay for educational expenses, and even though credit cards were easy for her to acquire and use, that they were not the best type of loan for her situation. It would have been a good idea for the young woman to talk to the financial aid department of her school about different options to finance her education, like student loans, instead of using credit cards.

This story also provides a basis for understanding how credit cards work, and the pitfalls when debt is not managed responsibly. It is clear from the story that the young woman does not understand the need to make payments to her credit card companies by the monthly deadlines. So she ends up owing a lot of money in late fees and punitive higher interest rates. All of those additional charges are compounded along with the interest owed on the balances that have accumulated through purchases made with the card, which makes her overall credit card balances—or amounts owed—skyrocket. When she starts to get into trouble with the cards, unable to pay even small amounts, the young woman in the story does not realize she needs to call the credit card companies to discuss her situation, and also meet with a credit counselor before her credit cards are turned over to collection agencies.

The video shows clearly to my students how compound interest—which is a key concept for both borrowing and saving/investing—can mean that minor differences in interest can increase exponentially over time. The video is a great lead-in to talking about how credit cards work, with different terms, payment contracts, and costs.

In addition to what can be learned from the credit horror story, in my classes I also teach students about credit scores, and how lending institutions use these numbers to gauge borrower riskiness and decide what interest to charge a borrower, or whether they will lend the money at all. We discuss how to build a credit history responsibly and how to start using credit carefully.

But we also talk about the idea that debt is not always a bad thing. That certain kinds of debt—depending on a broader analysis—might be a positive tool for a greater financial gain, when managed effectively. A couple of examples of these are mortgage debt and student loans. But we discuss these ideas with the caveat that all debt has to be managed responsibly and that it is not always easy to gauge the return from the cost of borrowing.

Credo Is Latin for . . .

So what are debt and credit, exactly, and how do they differ?

As discussed in Chapter 4 with budgeting, debt is the financial dynamic that occurs when you spend more than you earn. Debt is money owed and can exist in many different forms of loans. Most loans are directly related to what they are used to purchase, so they may be structured in different ways. Some loans, like home loans and car loans, have a component called "collateral." Collateral is an asset, like a house or a car, of approximately the same value as the loan, that is assigned to the lender if the loan is not repaid. For example, if a home loan is not repaid, the lender can take possession of the house that the loan was originally used to finance.

Here are some of the most common forms of consumer debt:

- *Credit cards.* Commonly known as "revolving" debt, credit cards allow the borrower to borrow money for discretionary and major expenses without any collateral, for possibly very high interest rates.
- *Consumer loans.* Money borrowed from a bank to pay for larger-than-normal expenses.
- *Car loans.* Funds borrowed to purchase a car. The loan can come from a bank or credit union, or any financial services firm, including one associated

directly with the car dealership. The loan is collateralized with the car, and if the loan is defaulted, the car can be repossessed by the lender in repayment of the loan.

- *Mortgages.* Home loan provided by a bank or credit union. Mortgages typically run 15 or 30 years and have more competitive rates as they are collateralized by the house. If the loan is defaulted, the lender can take possession of the house in repayment of the loan.

- *Student loans.* Funding provided by the government or private lenders like banks, for students to pay for college and other levels of education.

Debt in the form of loans typically has a cost, which is known as interest. The interest rate for a loan varies in terms of how risky the borrower is perceived to be, whether the loan is collateralized or not, the macroeconomic environment for interest rates, and possibly other factors, like the amount of the loan, or the length of time the loan will exist, which is also known as the term of the loan.

As we discussed in Chapter 5, interest rates can vary and can be simple or compounded interest. But what goes into the process for getting a loan? Meaning, how do lenders decide if they want to extend credit to a potential borrower?

Let's start with the meaning of the word "credit." Credit can mean a lot of different things to people.

Credit comes from the Latin word *credo,* or "to believe." In the financial services world, credit means that a lender, like a bank or a credit card company, believes you will repay the money you borrow, be it a mortgage, car loan, or credit card debt. Credit is about trust.

Every borrower is analyzed on the basis of how creditworthy she might be. Being a creditworthy borrower in the eyes of a lender means that the borrower is expected to repay a loan on time, in the period of time agreed to, and in the amount agreed to. This applies to borrowers who are governments, corporations, and individuals. So how can lenders measure creditworthiness, or the expectation that a loan will be repaid responsibly?

For individuals, one measure for creditworthiness is a credit score. The credit score is a compilation of an individual's credit history: a metric made up of information including how much you owe, what kind of debt you owe, if you have paid your previous debt back on time, and the length of your credit history. The more creditworthy you are, the more likely you will be able to borrow money, and at favorable rates. This analysis is historical, meaning, the assumption is made that however you behaved with credit in the past is how you will behave with credit—responsibly or irresponsibly—in the future.

Mortgages are a type of debt that women have struggled with in the past. Mortgages are critical in wealth development because most Americans' most significant asset is their house, and many of us cannot afford to buy a house without the assistance of a loan, or mortgage. The beauty of a mortgage is as you repay the loan, you own more of the house, which is also known as "building equity" in the house. Those who favor home ownership argue that you will have to pay to live anywhere, so why not pay each month into an asset where your ownership increases with each payment. This is in direct contrast with rent, where a payment is made usually each month to a landlord, and the tenant does not end up owning any percentage of the house or apartment. The tenant is paying for the service of living in the house or apartment, not paying off a mortgage and building equity.

However, mortgages can be structured to be complicated instruments, as was demonstrated clearly and tragically in the subprime mortgage crisis of 2008. At that time, some people had mortgages they did not understand, usually meaning that they did not understand how their monthly payments might change and ultimately could not afford to make the payments when they did increase. And during that crisis, women were shown to have received a disproportionate number of subprime mortgages compared to men, even when their credit scores were on a par with their male counterparts. Women also had a larger number of mortgage defaults and foreclosures.[1]

Creditworthiness Analysis: A Shortcut

So how is the creditworthiness of a borrower determined by a lender? It all begins with your credit history.

One critical concept for young people to understand is that their credit history begins as soon as they take out a loan of any kind, including a credit card, a student loan, a car loan, or other types of loans. The loans are associated with the borrower's social security number, as is the borrower's credit history. So when you take out your first loan, you have begun your credit history. This means that every payment you make—or don't make—is recorded with credit bureaus and is included in your credit score, which is a very important financial metric for banks and other entities.

A credit score is important because it is a snapshot of how risky a borrower you are—meaning, how likely it is that you will pay back a loan in full, and on time, based on your repayment behavior in the past. So credit managed from Day 1 can impact borrowing ability and costs, meaning interest rates, well beyond that time.

According to myFICO, a credit score is made up of the following components in these proportions:

- 35 percent—Payment history
- 30 percent—Amounts owed
- 15 percent—Length of credit history
- 10 percent—New credit
- 10 percent—Types of credit used[2]

Credit scores not only impact the ability to borrow and the interest level you pay for credit but can have significant life impact as they may be of interest to prospective employers and real estate brokers or landlords. Utility companies and cell phone providers may use your credit score to determine whether you need to make a deposit in order to get a contract.

In order to manage this all-important financial numeric, I teach students to do the following:

1. Understand the terms of all outstanding loans, and make the necessary payments in full, and on time.
2. Make sure your lenders have your current address. College kids and young twenties tend to move around a lot, but if your lender can't find you to send you a bill, statement, or other communication, it is not an excuse to miss payments.
3. Maintain communication with your lenders. If you have questions about the terms of your loan, ask your lender. If you are having trouble making a payment, call and find out what your options are.
4. Know your credit score. Check your score and credit history at least once a year.

There is a lot to know about managing credit—including managing how much you borrow. However, it is important that young people understand that once they start borrowing money in any form, they are beginning a credit history that will significantly impact their financial life now and in the future.

Invest in Yourself

The cost of credit is clear—when you borrow money, you have to repay it with interest, because money has a cost.

But there can be a potential upside, or value, to credit as well. Big corporations might borrow money as an investment in themselves. They can use the borrowed funds to expand, eventually hiring more people, producing more goods, and making a greater profit that may well be much higher than the cost of the credit was. The financial analysis done in this case is whether the benefit of the credit outstrips the cost. So how do you do the financial analysis to know if debt has a value? Although we will be covering more of these concepts in Chapter 7, the concept to understand when thinking about debt is actually the concept of "investing."

From a financial perspective, investing is putting money to work by buying something that you expect to earn more money from, meaning, it pays income or it will rise in value. The thing you pay for, for which you expect a positive "return" or gain in value, is an investment. Financial investments might include things like real estate or other financial instruments.

The same kind of analysis can be done by individuals. Take a mortgage, for example. How would you determine if a mortgage was a type of debt that was a good "investment." A mortgage, which is a home loan, allows you to buy a house with a down payment that is a fraction of the overall cost of the house, usually around 20 percent of the selling price. The homeowner then makes a monthly payment to the mortgage lender, just as she might make a rent payment to a landlord. The upside in this case is with each payment, more of the house is owned by the borrower/homeowner. Also, the value of the house may rise if the real estate market is strong. And the icing on this cake is that the mortgage interest is tax deductible (more on that in Chapter 8!).

The value of debt involves a financial analysis. It may also involve making a bet without all of the factors as yet knowable. In the examples above, the corporation may not definitely make a bigger profit with the debt-fueled expansion, and in the case of the homeowner, there is no guarantee the value of real estate will always go up. Although nothing in the financial markets is a sure thing, when used effectively, debt can be part of smart financial management.

But there is also such a thing as life investments. For example, we can all invest in ourselves and our human capital. Human capital is an economic term that means the intangible things we all have in ourselves that we can use to create economic value. For example, one way you can invest in yourself is to pay for more education that leads to a better paying job. In my classes, we look at a chart from the Bureau of Labor Statistics that shows clearly that education levels impact earning potential, with median weekly earnings increasing steadily in a range from "less than a high school diploma" to "high school diploma" to "bachelor's degree" and professional degrees. The chart indicates in no uncertain terms that education has a clear economic value for people.

I ask my students to compare the differences in income levels according to education. One comparison they seem to make automatically, as most of them are in high school working toward a diploma, but with an eye on college admission at some point in the relatively near future, is the high school diploma versus bachelor's degree.

They point out in the chart that the median weekly earnings for someone with a bachelor's degree is almost twice that of the median weekly earnings for someone with just a high school diploma. I usually then point out the other side of the chart, which is the unemployment rate categorized by different degree levels. In a similar comparison, the unemployment rate for people with only a high school diploma is almost twice that of a person with a bachelor's degree.

It is clear from this chart that education can be an investment in your human capital, an investment that can create greater economic value for a person. It is pretty clear that the investment in education is a good thing, but what if you can't afford to pay for college? Do you forgo the opportunity for this investment that seems pretty much guaranteed to provide you greater economic value in the future?

This dilemma presents an opportunity to discuss with my students the idea of debt as an investment. In the same way that a company borrows money to expand an assembly line to produce more products and potentially earn more money, people can do an analysis of when debt directed in a way that could yield greater economic value can be viewed as an investment.

Student loans have become increasingly common with the rising costs of college and other forms of higher education, and there is much talk about the burden of carrying the debt after college when trying to make it in the real world with a first-job salary. The real question then becomes, will the economic value the student loans bring in paying for college outweigh the costs of the loans to begin with? This analysis is critical—and not always simple—as all forms of college education do not cost the same, and all college degrees do not yield the same earning potential. However, it is worthwhile, and may yield consideration of opportunities like a two-year associate's degree followed by two years of four-year college, that cost only a fraction of the tuition of a private college but may yield a degree with similar earning potential.

Table 6.1   Credit Card Payoff Table

Current Balance	Interest Rate (APR)	Minimum Payment	Payoff Period (in Months)	Total Paid	Interest Paid (Total Paid— Current Balance)
$1,000	8.99%	$30 (3%)	68 months		
$1,000	14.99%	$30 (3%)	82 months		
$1,000	24.99%	$30 (3%)	132 months		
$2,000	8.99%	$100 (5%)	65 months		
$2,000	14.99%	$100 (5%)	72 months		
$2,000	24.99%	$100 (5%)	90 months		
$5,000	14.99%	$200 (4%)	123 months		
$5,000	24.99%	$200 (4%)	169 months		

Do Try This at Home!

Debt is incurred when you spend more money than you earn and use money that is not your own—it might be a loan from the bank, a credit card balance, a loan for a car or a house, or any other kind of borrowed money.

Although debt, or borrowed money, can seem like a positive as it may help you achieve something you really want, like home ownership or a college education, as we have discussed throughout the chapter, it is important to recognize that money has a cost. And as we have also learned, that cost is known as "interest." Interest is the rent paid on money that you borrow from other people and institutions, usually expressed as a percentage of the total amount borrowed.

This activity is focused on figuring out how long it will take to pay off a credit card in eight different scenarios, as well as how much extra will be paid, when a minimum payment is made and interest is accumulating. We do this with the Credit Card Payoff Table (Table 6.1). We even include an answer key for the activity (Table 6.2)!

In some cases when the balance and interest rates are high, when a minimum payment is made each month, more than twice the original balance is paid back. This shows the power of compound interest as the interest paid is equal to or higher than the original balance borrowed.

Table 6.2   Credit Card Payoff Table Answer Key

Current Balance	Interest Rate (APR)	Minimum Payment	Payoff Period (in Months)	Total Paid	Interest Paid (Total Paid— Current Balance)
$1,000	8.99%	$30 (3%)	68 months	$1,243.78	$243.78
$1,000	14.99%	$30 (3%)	82 months	$1,507.37	$507.37
$1,000	24.99%	$30 (3%)	132 months	$2,496.88	$1,496.88
$2,000	8.99%	$100 (5%)	65 months	$2,325.84	$325.84
$2,000	14.99%	$100 (5%)	72 months	$2,613.50	$613.50
$2,000	24.99%	$100 (5%)	90 months	$3,305.55	$1,305.55
$5,000	14.99%	$200 (4%)	123 months	$7,177.56	$2,177.56
$5,000	24.99%	$200 (4%)	169 months	$7,177.56	$2,177.56

Discussion Points

Although credit scores and mortgages may not be the right place to start discussing debt with all ages, here are some tips about how to talk about debt with daughters of a range of ages:

1. What is debt? Debt is the money that you owe when you spend more money than you have. It can take lots of forms, like credit card debt, or loans for cars, homes, or education.
2. How can you avoid spending more money than you have? Determine your spending "needs" versus "wants" and learn how to keep a budget. Record your spending to figure out where your money is going.
3. How can you afford to buy something without borrowing? If there is a big purchase you want but cannot currently afford, put together a plan for saving and earning the money over time so you can buy the item that you want at some point in the future.
4. Is borrowing money always a bad thing? Not necessarily. But when you do borrow money, you need to be sure to try to keep your borrowing costs as low as possible, understand the terms of the repayment, and make sure you pay back the money in the amount you promise, in the amount of time you say you will.

MANAGING CREDIT AND DEBT

1. Understand how to have a strong credit history and a good credit score.
2. Learn how to determine the cost of credit.
3. Think about how debt can sometimes be an investment and how to measure the value versus the cost of the debt.

CHAPTER SEVEN

Investing: Girls Don't Need to Fall Behind

Introduction

Investing is a hot topic when I teach it to my high school- and college-level classes. These young women come to class knowing bits and pieces about stocks, bonds, and markets, and are very motivated to put all the pieces together and solve the puzzle, and make some money! And I love teaching about investing, as it gets to the heart of financial confidence and engagement. However, investing is an area that I found in my research where women need more education, and I see this to be true in real life.

What does it mean to invest, and why is investing so important for women? An investment is something that you buy with the expectation it will gain value over time. That change in value is known as the return on the investment, and can be positive or negative, and is usually expressed as a percentage. If the return is positive, investing can grow your money over a period of time.

Investing can be particularly important for women since, as we have discussed in this book, women earn less than men on average and also outlive their male counterparts.[1] Finding additional mechanisms to build wealth can help women become more able to care for themselves and their families financially. However, studies have shown consistently that women tend to be risk-averse, to a fault, when it comes to investing.[2] The "fault" issue has to do with the need to invest in risky, "growth" assets like stocks that provide the potential for a higher return, in order to build wealth over time for life needs like retirement. This damaging risk aversion is related to a lack of confidence women have in themselves in this crucial area.

But there is a lot to learn in the area of investing that can help young women continue to gain confidence and acumen in this area. It is important to understand different assets classes for consumers, like stocks and bonds, as well as different tools for managing risk, like diversification and asset allocation. Additionally, although it is critical to be empowered with knowledge about investing, and a disposition to be willing to take the necessary risk to grow wealth sufficiently, the right expert can provide much-needed support and partnership in this area. But first, we need to make sure our young women understand the importance of investing for women.

So how do we keep the investing interest and engagement alive in young women so it carries forward to a time when they are earning, and they actually have the need and ability to invest? We need to start talking to these young women about investing now, so that they can help build their confidence and capability, and eventually, their engagement. In my classes, I show my students how to invest and encourage them to start investing now, even with very modest sums. This experience demystifies investment and helps to keep interest and engagement alive until such time as these girls are earning money and have a greater ability to invest.

Financial Nutrition® Method

- *Money as commodity*
- *Risk*
- *Value*
- *Opportunity costs*
- *Information*

Investing is at the crux of the concepts underlying the Financial Nutrition® Method. Put simply, investing is making money with money, so in that case money is clearly a *commodity*. The sole purpose of investing is to grow wealth, and that wealth is grown by utilizing money to buy different investments that will increase in value.

Investing is also fraught with *risk*—there are typically no guarantees and always a chance that things will go badly. Risk is a critical part of investing, and at the same time, an important dynamic in making money with investing. Risk can be measured in terms of price volatility, meaning the potential for the price of an asset to move up and down, or fluctuate.

These fluctuations provide opportunities to both make money and lose money. But along with the risk of loss does come the opportunity for gain.

Successful investing entails finding *value*, pure and simple, or finding something that grows in value. The best investments are those that are undervalued, meaning, the market has not yet figured out what the investment is worth, although you may have. Of course this analysis is not simple or without risk. However, finding value in investing is a potential way to be successful.

Investing also involves *opportunity costs*, when buying one investment is potentially the opportunity forgone of owning another investment. As was discussed in earlier chapters, money can only be spent on one thing at a time. So buying one investment means you cannot buy a different one with the same money—you have to choose. Similarly, opportunity costs present themselves when money is used elsewhere, and then not available to be put in the market.

And finally, *information* may be one of the most valuable elements of successful investing. Information can be the difference between losing and winning in investing, as information allows the investor to make the proper analysis of what is a good investment. Although there are no "sure things" with investing, having good information about an investment can help an investor do better analysis about the likelihood of the success of an investment.

The Financial Nutrition® Method also attempts to deal with the disposition of women toward investment—the engagement, the risk aversion, the concern about working with experts. In this way, investing is an example of a financial area where the Financial Nutrition® Method can make a huge difference in women's financial success.

Are Girls Engaged with Investing?

Are girls interested in investing? Good question. Because interest usually means—or at least leads to—engagement, learning, even expertise and success. And investing is important for building wealth over time, saving for big-ticket items like college or retirement. In other words, investing is a way to make money with money and supplement whatever other earnings are coming in, like a paycheck or an inheritance.

The truth is, investing is pretty complicated for everyone. It can also be scary, as there is a potential to lose money. Sometimes an interest in or success with investing comes down to whether or not people enjoy it. Some studies show that men think investing is fun and that women find it stressful. The fun aspect for men does not necessarily make them better investors, however. In fact, sometimes investing is so much fun for men that they end up trading too much, meaning buying and selling stocks, for example, and incurring transaction costs. The transaction costs eat into any profit they might make. With this buying and selling, the timing is not always right, which means buying high and selling low. This combination of transaction costs and poor timing can mean that men actually end up earning less than women, who might be white-knuckling it through the whole experience and holding on to investments out of fear.[3]

I have found investing to be a pretty popular topic in my financial education classes for girls. This is evidenced by their attention when I begin the initial explanations like what is a stock, what is a bond, what is risk. They usually listen with rapt attention as if they knew this was a topic that will impact their lives greatly, and they ask intelligent, engaging questions, showing that they are paying attention and want to go further.

First we discuss the basics. What is a stock, I ask? A piece of a company. So, I say, if I own a share of Facebook, can I fly out to Mountain View, California, march into the lobby, and demand to see Founder and CEO Mark Zuckerberg? Nope. Why not? Because companies that sell stock to the public—known as publicly traded companies—means we can all own a small part. Unless we own a big part, we don't have any power inside the company. We just get to watch our investment grow in value if the stock price increases, or the opposite if the price goes down.

But where I really see the girls' interest in investing is in an activity we do after we cover the basics of investing. After we discuss the basics, like stocks, bonds, diversification, asset allocation, risk, and liquidity, I ask the students to break up into teams and come up with well-diversified model portfolios. The goal of the activity is to have each team come up with a portfolio, or group of investments, that individually have potential to increase in value and are also not similar to each other. The diversification means that the group contains assets that differ across different categories.

Now remember, at the most, they have only had a couple of hours of class on the topic of investing. But what happens next is truly remarkable, and makes me believe—as if I did not already—that women have the potential to be extremely savvy, engaged, successful investors.

First, there's the enthusiasm. The girls break up into teams and usually whip out their phones, or flip open their laptops, to start googling different investment ideas. There is a buzz and a palpable energy in the room, as each team debates different ideas, and each student voices her opinion in the group. As I walk around the room, listening in on their active discussions about different companies, I realize that these girls have a much greater awareness of the companies that are the building blocks of the U.S. economy. They know the old-guard companies, the hot new companies, and everything in between.

What is even more impressive than their clear knowledge of individual companies is their ability to build carefully constructed, creatively diversified portfolios. Again, these students have only had a couple of hours of learning on the topic of investing. But nevertheless, they come up with ideas utilizing different kinds of stocks, funds, private equity, and even commodities. They are strategic and intelligent in their thinking, and clearly very interested and engaged, and demonstrating an absolute ability to be activist and successful in their investing lives.

When the teams have designed their portfolio, each team takes turns sending a representative to the board to write down the list of investments in the team's portfolio. Then as a class we provide constructive feedback—what we think works in each portfolio presented and what we think might not be as successful a choice. In this way, the students learn to both present and articulate their ideas, and also provide helpful ideas about how to improve the portfolio. They learn from each other, and the enthusiasm and learning move forward at a dynamic pace.

Women and Investing: What's Missing?

Women have a few strikes against them when it comes to investing. First, there's the issue of risk aversion, which prevents some women from investing effectively in the riskier assets that will truly offer the potential to grow their wealth over time. As we know from the gender wage gap, women have less access to capital, which manifests in earning less and saving less. When you have less money to begin with, you have less money to lose, so it's not always easy to take risks with what you have. Risk is a critical concept for women, because women are challenged financially.

Risk impacts women on the investing side, not just in the money that they spend for money but the money they earn on their money. Women's demonstrated aversion to risk in investing can hurt them financially. A certain amount of risk is necessary in order to earn returns that can grow the type of wealth we will all need in retirement. That is why it is particularly important for women to understand the risk-return relationship and how it applies to investing.

Women also can approach their investing, in the context of overall wealth management, differently than men. Research shows that women tend to view their wealth more holistically, with human priorities in addition to financial ones.[4] Although this may not sound "rational" according to old-school, nonbehavioral economics, it is the approach women may take.

Does this disposition of a more holistic approach to wealth management hurt the investor, or financial well-being in general? No. In fact, when it comes to investing, it is important that the way money is invested fits into a holistic wealth management plan.

For example, let's start with the age-old question, "Is this a good investment?" Although that is not a bad question to ask, it is impossible to answer it without an understanding and examination of the bigger picture of a financial life, including goals for the future.

Managing money—and eventually wealth—needs to be done holistically, all different elements of a financial life aligned. Many people take an a la carte approach to their money, keeping separate their spending, investing, taxes, and estate planning. They may even keep investments in separate parts of their brain or not even know what they own. I have heard more than one person say, "I think I have a 401(k), but I'm not really sure what investments it contains."

And eventually there's the inevitable question or sales pitch of a new investment product, or a friend who is all gung ho about a new approach to whole life insurance or certain tax deductions. But no matter how much money you have, your wealth planning and management needs to fit into a bigger picture of how much money you have, how much you need, your overall life goals, where you are in your life, and many other factors. You can't evaluate a new investment simply on its own merits because of the need to incorporate it into your personal bigger picture: your financial goals, time for investing, and asset allocation for diversification. And your investment portfolio alone is not even the whole picture when it comes to building wealth.

Interestingly, women do seem to look at investing more in the bigger picture of their life's goals, hopes, fears, children.[5] And in the end it makes a lot of sense, and is a very savvy approach. When investing, goals are necessary to guide the process—how much do you need to earn and save and by when? For a house? For your retirement? For your children or other legacy? For the donations you feel passionate about?

Your wealth accumulation and planning is also going to be impacted by how you protect it with tools like insurance and tax planning. If the biggest input to your wealth accumulation is your income, then maximizing your income is critical. Are you earning as much as you can in the job you have? Would another job be more enjoyable and lucrative, and what are the costs and benefits of attaining it?

When I teach girls about money, I teach them a broad range of financial understanding. In class we talk about budgeting and financial planning, income and salary negotiations, saving and investing, and taxes and insurance. We focus on risk and value, and look at opportunity costs. We talk about the importance of experts, and self-education and engagement with money.

So the big picture of money is truly a big picture. It involves income and investment management, tax and insurance planning, and estate planning and philanthropy. When one piece falls out, the picture is incomplete, and your wealth and what you would like to share with others is at risk.

A certain peace can come with the holistic approach because, all of a sudden, everything has a purpose and a logic. Decisions about money can be made as part of a system that is clearly defined and understood. And most importantly, everything from your spending to investing to tax management is working in concert to achieve what is most important now and in the future, for you and those you care about.

This may sound complicated, but no one has to go it alone when it comes to financial planning and investing. But women face barriers in this area too. Hand and hand with the positive disposition to approach wealth management more holistically, research shows, is a general discomfort women have with the way they are treated in the financial services industry.[6] We will explore working with experts further in Chapter 11, but in the context of learning about investing, it is worth pointing out that women do not tend to work with experts and it prevents some of the learning, and ultimately, success that they may have had with investing.

So How Does Investing Work?

Investing is making money with money, simply put. The goal with investing is to purchase some sort of an asset and hope that it grows in value over time, so you can potentially sell it at some point in the future and make a profit. The adage "buy low, sell high" covers this idea perfectly.

Investing can be done with all sorts of things like property, art, even cars. But the way most people in the United States grow their wealth through investing is in the financial markets. The financial markets are simply markets where financial investments, like stocks and bonds, are sold. Financial markets, like all markets, bring together buyers and sellers, and as a result of different forces like supply and demand, prices are set by the market.

In the universe of all of the different financial assets, most consumers tend to invest mainly in stocks, bonds, and mutual funds. Here is a quick explanation of each of these financial instruments:

- *Stocks.* Stocks, also known as equities, are issued by publicly held companies and are basically a piece of the company. Investors make money when the value of the stock increases, and is then sold. Stock prices usually increase when the company's earnings increase, or when they are expected to increase.
- *Bonds.* Bonds, also known as fixed income, are loans made by investors to the borrowing company. Bonds are issued through deals done by investment banks and are sold in allocations typically of $1,000. They frequently pay an interest rate, known as a coupon, two times per year. They also have specific terms, and usually at the end of a term, or maturity, the bondholder gets the full value of the bond, or principal, paid back.
- *Mutual funds.* Mutual funds are investments that pool the funds of multiple investors, and with that money, the fund manager will buy a variety of investments, like stocks or bonds. Investors can buy into the fund with a small amount of money and gain exposure to all of the assets in the fund.

In addition to knowing the basics of available consumer investment products, a couple of very important dynamics of investing need to be understood as a foundation—risk and diversification.

Risk is the possibility that something bad will happen. With investing, risk means the possibility of losing some or all of your original investment. Risk can be scary, for sure, and it can be easy to just choose to avoid it all together. But while investments with low risk may not have far to fall because their prices don't change that much, their stability also means they do not have far to climb. This means you do not have the same potential to make money. Investments that are more volatile—meaning, their prices fluctuate more wildly—provide more of an opportunity to make money in the swings between the prices. Think, buy low, sell high—the prices of volatile assets will hit higher and lower points than less risky assets. What makes the assets risky is that it's hard to know how and when the asset price will move in a different direction.

Not investing in risky assets can be a risk for women, because they earn less, save less, and live longer than men. Women need to take a sufficient amount of risk in investing to help provide the possibility of growing enough wealth for retirement and other purposes. And while it is impossible to manage away all the risk in any portfolio because markets are too unpredictable, there are approaches that can help mitigate risk.

One way is diversification—meaning, don't put all your eggs in one basket, as the old adage says. The underlying idea is that if you spread your money around to different kinds of assets, the prices may not all fall at the same time. Although some prices may fall, the idea is that overall and over time your portfolio will gain in value. Diversification can be done within asset classes. For example, there are different kinds of stocks, both in terms of the size of companies (small-cap, mid-cap, and large-cap), and the different industries that companies can belong to, like technology and health care. So, investors can diversify by buying different sized companies, or companies in different industries, among other options. Diversification can also be done across different asset classes. For example, investors can invest in different types of assets like stocks, bonds, as well as real estate, and other asset classes.

So how do you diversify? Here are some basic approaches:

Across Asset Classes

An asset class is a type of investment, like a stock. Different investments behave differently, have different levels of volatility, or change in price, and respond differently to market conditions. Consumers typically diversify across asset classes by investing in stocks, bonds, and cash. Another class of investments is known as "alternative investments," which are typically more the purview of sophisticated investors, like institutions, as they are more complicated to analyze, and there may be income regulations as to who can legally invest in them. Alternative investments include hedge funds, private equity, real estate, and commodities.

Within Asset Classes

Diversification does not just end with asset classes; in fact, additional diversification can happen within a type of asset. Stocks are a great example of how this can be done. Not all companies' shares behave the same way. Diversification can happen across large and small companies, like older, more established companies and new, high-growth businesses. Investors can also diversify with U.S. and international companies.

Diversification can further be achieved across different kinds of companies, also known as sectors, in the stock market. Energy, health care, and telecommunications are all examples of different market sectors.

With Human Capital

You can even diversify your investments with your income stream. If you are working at a high-risk start-up with a great potential for gain or loss, you may want to consider investments that are more stable and dependable. Or, if your company offers you a retirement fund with a lot of the company stock, think about diversifying into other investments to ensure your fortune is not tied to the company in both current income and retirement savings.

No investment is a sure thing, so some risk is typically necessary to make money from investing. Diversifying your assets can be a way to help lower risk but still earn the return you need to help meet life's financial challenges.

Here are a few more valuable components that can contribute to successful investing:

- *Time, time, time.* Time is a huge asset when it comes to investing. Not only does time allow you to benefit from the power of compounding—earning returns on returns—it allows you to ride out market cycles. Markets don't always go up, and they don't always go down. They do both, and timing the market has proven to be difficult. But if you can leave your money invested for a long period of time, you have greater potential to ride out the down cycles and grow more wealth.

- *Working with an expert.* It's important to know the market and understand the economy so that you can trust your instinct when it comes to investing. However, you do not have to be an expert. We all have our areas of expertise, and you don't have to be an expert in all things. But if you're not an investment expert, you may want to work with someone who is. When you do look for an expert, find one who provides what you need—solid expertise and a proven track record, and a style that is comfortable for you, as well as all the information you want. This relationship is a very important one, so make sure you feel good about it, and don't hire someone until you do.

- *Cost management.* When you work with an expert, whether it's someone who manages money for you personally or manages a mutual fund that you invest in, there will be costs involved like commissions and expenses. These costs are how money managers get paid. But costs vary, and they should relate to the value the expert or fund is providing. So, if a manager or fund is expensive but their performance is not good, it's a low-value proposition. Remember—you are not making money for yourself until your investment gains have covered the costs of that investment, including the fees of the manager.

- *Education and engagement.* Education and engagement with your money in all areas is critical. For investing, it is important to make sure you educate yourself on an ongoing basis, including self-education through books and media, or formal education through classes, or working closely with an expert. Engagement means monitoring your money, the markets, and the economy, and staying in touch with your financial adviser if you have one. It's important to understand what is happening in the world and how it is impacting your money.

You Have to Learn This Now!

As parents, we do our best to teach our children things we know, to the best of our ability. But some things are harder to talk about than others, and investing, in some cases, is one of the harder things.

I had a student who came to class one day, and during our opening discussion, she talked about her father feeling a desperate need to impart to her an understanding of investing. He was very busy with work and travel, but when he did have time, he would attempt to teach her everything he knew about investing, in mere minutes. My student mentioned that once he came to school to bring her something she had left at home and took the five minutes they were together to give her a quick tutorial on stocks!

Another student mentioned that her father had a more measured, methodical approach . . . with her brother. The student said that her interest in investing tended to fluctuate, but that her brother was always an avid investing learner. So their father had developed a habit where he would give the brother books about investing principles and speak with him directly about the family's investments, often leaving her out.

Investing is a complicated topic, and it can be challenging to find the time to discuss it and to make sure parents are aware of children's interests. But we have a few ideas for girls to learn about investing, and for families to discuss this complicated topic.

Do Try This at Home!

The best way to learn about investing is to actually follow markets, or at least individual stocks. With so much financial information available on the Internet, it can be easy to find plenty of information to track a company and get a sense of how stock prices move up and down, and how to find value.

For this exercise, start by finding three publicly traded companies that you are interested in, or that you think have the potential to increase their profits, or earnings, in the near future. These companies would need to have a strong management, a competitive product, and a solid business approach. Once you find the three companies, do the following:

- Go to a financial website like Bloomberg.com and do a news search on the company. Read some of the significant stories of the past three years. If you find anything that makes you think perhaps the company is not so good, replace that company with a better one.

- Check the stock price over the past year and past five years. How has it been performing? Is it going straight up, or is it all over the place, or perhaps headed straight down? See how this makes you feel about owning the company.
- Finally, follow the stock price for the next few months, and see if the price goes in the direction you expected it to.

Discussion Points

Here are some additional discussion points you can share with the young woman in your life about how to become engaged and literate in the dynamics of investing. Financial conversations using these discussion points can be had whenever is convenient—at breakfast, in the car, during family time, or a specially prescribed time to talk about money in a group or a club.

1. *Risk.* With investing, there is risk, which means the possibility that things will go badly, and you will lose money. Investors need to be prepared for that and also learn mechanisms for helping to mitigate risk.
2. *Diversification.* This is a tool to help manage risk, along the lines of the old axiom "don't put all of your eggs in one basket." If you invest across different types of asset classes (likes stocks and bonds), and diversify within asset classes (like different sectors or parts of the world), you have less of a chance of losing everything as your investments likely will not all decline at once.
3. *Educate yourself.* Start learning about the world and markets now. Find a respectable daily news publication and read it religiously. Economies and markets tend to move in cycles—once you follow the story, you will see it happening over and over again.

HOW TO START INVESTING

1. Choose companies you have heard of that look to be successful.
2. Research the company and analyze recent news about it.
3. Follow the past and future price movements.

CHAPTER EIGHT

Taxes Don't Have to Be a Dirty Word

Introduction

Taxes. A pretty grim topic according to most people! For many, the overarching sentiment about taxes—other than fear, anxiety, and dread, is certainty, as exemplified by this quote from Christopher Bullock in 1716 in *The Cobbler of Preston*: "'Tis impossible to be sure of any thing but Death and Taxes."[1]

Why are taxes so scary, to put it mildly? Why do most people dread that famous deadline in the United States of April 15, when tax returns are due to the government? I would wager the primary reason is that taxes are not easy to understand, but at the same time, cost us money, and if not handled properly, can cost us even more money. All of this can make paying taxes very stressful to most people.

Why are taxes so hard to understand? Taxes are difficult to understand because they involve formulas that can be complex and opaque, laws that an ordinary person would not know and that change as frequently as each year, and because the whole concept of taxation might be at odds with a person's value system, meaning they do not think taxes are fair for one or a variety of reasons, which can create another barrier of understanding. Additionally, taxes are another one of those financial things that many people believe are understood and gamed by people who have more money, and that "regular" people will never completely understand them, and in a sense, will be taken advantage of, ultimately resulting in paying more than their fair share.

Another tricky aspect to taxes is that they involve careful and effective financial record-keeping. Careful and effective financial record-keeping goes right back to the need to be intentional with money—knowing and understanding what you spend and keeping track of it. Taking a step back specifically in the context of taxes, knowing specifically what you need to know and the records you need to keep and save. Adding a strategic, mental twist, knowing how best to spend your money so that your tax hit is as low as possible, which then requires a level of expertise and understanding that might need to change every year as the tax laws change, or if you move to a different state, or into a house, or start investing.

So now we understand why taxes are scary, but what are taxes, really?

Taxes, to put it simply, are charges by the government to the people to pay for shared public goods, including paying the salaries of those same government officials. Paying taxes is required by law and differ sometimes from state to state and country to country. In the United States, we have a variety of different taxes including:

- *Earned income tax.* Tax paid as a percentage of the income you earn, and can be paid to the national government (known as federal tax), state, and city governments.
- *Capital gains tax.* Tax paid on the profits earned from investments.
- *Property tax.* Tax paid on property like houses and usually used to pay for schools.
- *Inheritance tax.* Tax paid on money inherited.
- *Sales tax.* Taxes paid on goods purchased, which can vary from state to state.

So, the confusion can start even in understanding which type of tax is which, without even knowing how they are calculated, and what a person's individual responsibility is for paying them.

At this point, you may think that there are so many taxes that you will have to pay in your life, that you do not even want to read on! But rest assured there is a solution to understanding and managing taxes—tax planning and tax preparation are not something you have to do alone. In fact, with the exception of accountants and tax attorneys, few people know everything there is to know about the tax code, as it changes every year. Taxes are definitely an area where it makes sense to hire a trusted expert, because the value assessment is clear—using a professional to do one's taxes frequently saves more money in tax efficiency than it costs in accounting fees.

My overarching goal in teaching about taxes is to help girls understand that taxes don't have to arouse anxiety and fear, but are rather simply a financial output that needs to be considered and managed, whether they are income based, taxes on property or inheritance, or capital gains on investments. Understanding how taxes work and planning financial structures strategically to avoid paying more taxes than necessary are also ways of being intentional with money, and ways to help grow wealth by managing tax costs effectively.

Taxes can be a dreaded part of life for many of us. They are just one of those things that cause anxiety. But if you understand how taxes work and how to make the most of your income and tax strategies, it can be an empowering experience. This is another area where it can really help to work with an expert, like an accountant. If you work with someone who collaborates with you, you will be empowered to take control of your financial life, including planning your taxes over time so that the strategy helps you financially and is no longer a source of pain and anxiety.

Financial Nutrition® Method: Activating the Value of Information

- *Money as commodity*
- Risk
- *Value*
- Opportunity costs
- *Information*

Managing taxes effectively is basically the same thing as managing your money. Going back to the concept of money as a *commodity*, how you structure your financial life to manage the ensuing tax burden effectively is transferring the potential expenditure of money on taxes to something else in your life, like an investment or a new car. Voila—money as a commodity!

With taxes, the concepts of *value* and *information* pretty much collide, meaning that there is value in the information that can help you manage your tax burden efficiently. Information like what expenditures are deductible, how to use a tax-deferred retirement plan, and other similar issues can help you save money on your taxes. The issue with taxes is there is information that is certain. Information is critical in investing too, but no matter how much information you have with investing there will always be unknowns, which means risk is always there, and things can go badly.

Taxes, on the other hand, live in a world where information is finite and accessible, and hence, of great value. This does not necessarily mean that the information is easy to understand or follow or that it does not change year after year, but the fact is, the information is codified and static for a period. This means that understanding taxes, and potentially working with an accountant or adviser who *really* understands taxes and has a grasp of all of the finite information available, has huge value that translates clearly into money you can save, money that you might not be able to save without that grasp of information.

I'll Make How Much after Taxes? Wait, What??!!

When I work with teenaged girls, one of the biggest shocks, or "aha" moments, is when we talk about taxes, in the context of budgeting and income. We do a budgeting exercise early on as the foundation of learning in a number of areas. One of the biggest challenges with teaching teenagers and the younger set is that so much about money is abstract to them—at least the big money issues. Young people cannot have their own credit cards, mortgages, or car loans, and typically have very small sums of money to manage.

Money learning, as we have discussed, is very experiential. It is experiential both from a learning perspective—meaning, the understanding sticks better if it is gained through the experience of actually managing money, but also from an engagement perspective. Specifically, money learning tends to be more engaging the more "real" that it is. So, with young people, it is a good idea to do simulations, or other sorts of exercises, where they actually get to manage money. They get to think of their hopes and dreams and plans for the future, and put pen to paper, and work to figure out how this life can be created, or sustained, from a financial perspective.

So, going back to the budgeting exercise, we work from a chart that has "Income" at the top, and "Expenses" at the bottom. In this exercise, some expenses are fixed, and taxes are one of those expenses. We move through the chart by first talking about income, and how much that is, on a gross, or total level. Then we move down to the next section, "Expenses," and that's where the first learning about taxes sometimes hits.

As the girls examine the number, and it dawns on them that the salary they negotiated in an earlier class does not translate into the amount of money they will actually take home each month and have to spend on their hopes, dreams, and the lives they want to create, a variety of responses come out. The take-home salary people have is less the amount they have to pay in taxes each month.

When my students learn that taxes will take away a percentage of their hard-earned income each month before they have had a chance to spend or save any of it, they are not very happy. Surprise, anger, confusion, and wonder usually top the chart of emotional responses for that part of the exercise. As I have taught my classes many times in New York City, I go on to point out that with federal, state, and city taxes, a worker in New York City may possibly only take home 50 percent of the salary that she earned.

So we move from this emotional, angry place of financial realization, to a short civics lesson. Let's talk about this, I say, let's take a look at what taxes in the United States are used for. Who knows why we are taxed and what tax revenue is used for by the government?

Usually there is some confusion around sales tax versus all the other kinds, which I clear up, as sales tax and earned income tax are different animals. So, going back to the big hit of taxes on a budget, I ask again, what are taxes in the United States used for? The students think and start to chime in: roads, police, fire fighters, parks, defense, public schools, sidewalks, bridges, highways . . . The list goes on! At this point the conversation can take more of a political turn, with the girls expressing their own, or possibly their parents' opinions about whether our tax dollars are used effectively or efficiently.

This is an important conversation, for sure, but the focus is financial, so I pull the conversation back to money. But what is critical—and what happened in this exercise—is that the girls understood, in no uncertain terms, that they have an inescapable financial responsibility that they will have to factor in to their budgets throughout their lives, as they build a financial life to support their hopes and dreams.

How We Create Wealth and Meaning: The Tax Context for Women

Let's look at some of the ways people in the United States create wealth. We work, first of all, and earn money and save and invest some of that money. We own homes, building equity through paying down the mortgage we may have taken out in order to afford the house. We invest money in the financial markets. And some of us inherit money from earlier generations of our families. All of these forms of income are impacted by taxes, whether it's income tax at the federal, state, and local levels; capital gains taxes on investments and home value appreciation; or inheritance tax. So for whatever form of income we make or have, some attention needs to be paid to managing the tax cost of that income.

Women are in a unique position when it comes to understanding and managing their taxes, for two simple—but critical—reasons. First, as we discussed earlier in this book, women earn less compared to men, save less, and are almost twice as likely to end their lives below the poverty line. In this context of lower wealth, as we have discussed, women also continue to take on greater and greater responsibility for the economic care of their families. So it is important to manage the cost side of the wealth equation as effectively as possible, whether it's budgeting and credit or taxes. Given this context of even scarcer resources, women do not have the room to pay any more than they absolutely have to in taxes. Understanding taxes and figuring out effective tax management on your own or with an expert is a key and critical part of women's effective financial management and empowerment.

What you actually earn from working and investing can be severely impacted by taxes, and if you are doing anything out of the ordinary in your income production—like contract work instead of a salaried position—efficient tax structures become even more critical to preserving income. As the U.S. economy continues to evolve, we work in lots of different ways, not just in the traditional, life-long, full-time work for a corporation or nonprofit organization where a salary increases each year by about the same percentage. Americans work part-time, sometimes combining multiple part-time or seasonal jobs. They own their own businesses. They work full-time in the formal economy. They move in and out of the workforce.

And all of these trends that are true for Americans are even more true for women. Although women make up about half of the U.S. workforce now,[2] some interesting trends exist that are likely not going away. Although most men and women who work in the United States do so on a full-time basis, women are twice as likely as men to work in the world of part-time work.[3] Although working part-time potentially provides some time flexibility, some financial deficits may also exist, besides the fact that part-time workers are likely earning less than full-time workers because they work fewer hours. Other financial hits revolve around the lack of benefits that may be paid to part-time workers, like health care benefits, paid vacation and sick time, and employer-provided retirement funds. These benefits that might be provided as part of the compensation of a full-time worker are instead costs that have to be incurred by a part-time worker who is already working, and possibly earning, less. This is a clear scenario where women need to manage the cost of taxes as effectively as possible, as they are more likely to work part-time.

Women are also owning their own businesses at a high rate over time. Between 2007 and 2016, the number of women-owned businesses increased by 45 percent, and women are majority owners of an increasing number of businesses.[4] Being a business owner, or even an independent contractor, offers different potential structures for paying taxes. In fact, businesses can be very tax-efficient vehicles if taxes are handled properly and appropriately. Some women work on a full- or part-time basis with a business or contract work on the side. This work structure presents even more complications and opportunities to manage the tax burden. Women also move in and out of the workforce more frequently than men, creating financial and tax complications.

However you decide to work, and build your life to achieve your dreams, it is clear that effective tax planning is key in the overall income and wealth building picture. In the planning, you can learn basic strategies and approaches to effective tax management.

Tax Analysis and Strategy

Tax planning is a critical piece of wealth management, at any level. No matter whether you work full- or part-time, you are the CEO of your own business or an artist, or just do some consulting work on the side of a full-time job, you can manage your taxes sensibly and effectively. You need to be activist in your tax planning.

A few things to consider are how you are compensated and what you do in your life that might effectively lower your income. One way to lower your tax costs is by having deductions to your income. A deduction is something that has been deemed by the Internal Revenue Service, or IRS, which is the government tax authority in the United States, to be able to be subtracted from your income and not bear a tax. Although a deduction does not lower the taxes owed by the amount of the deduction, it does lower the amount of income that is taxed by the amount of the deduction. So deductions help you pay less tax in the amount of the percentage of tax you typically pay, multiplied by the deduction amount.

Some common deductions include the interest paid on a mortgage, professional fees and costs related to a job, moving costs, children, investing losses, taxes paid the previous year, professional fees paid to an accountant, and donations to charity. In order to utilize deductions effectively in your tax planning, it is important to (1) know what expenditure qualifies as a deduction, (2) know what kind of deductions you have, and (3) keep track of them throughout the year.

Careful tax planning, like deductions, shows the need to not treat financial management as an afterthought, nor with an a la carte approach, keeping separate things like spending, investing, philanthropy, and taxes. Because income taxes might be as high as 50 percent of the income you earn, it is important to think about structuring your financial life with an eye toward your goals and dreams, but in a financially holistic way, where all of the components work together. This is the same idea as was discussed in Chapter 7 about holistic wealth management.

Let's look at what this means in a specific case. You may have a lot of goals in your life:

•   Earning a certain amount of money to take care of yourself and your family
•   Having enough money to retire comfortably
•   Giving back to the world in a focused, charitable way

Those three things all fit together as part of your financial picture, and all of them have tax ramifications. However, the good news is that you can use different aspects of each to offset the overall taxes you pay.

Let's start with the first item on the list, earning enough money to take care of yourself and your family. This may be your primary source of income, so the main goal here is to protect it, and try to earn as much as you can in net income, or income after taxes. As we discussed in Chapter 3, you can also potentially increase your salary by negotiating effectively or working in certain fields that pay more on average. That is working on your wealth from the income side and is certainly important and can be an effective approach to earning as much as possible in all different types of work situations.

Managing your taxes in this case is the same thing as managing costs in other areas of your life. So in order to have higher net income, you need to pay lower taxes. In this scenario, the second two goals can help the tax management of the first one.

Let's look next at saving for retirement. The IRS allows certain types of retirement savings to be tax deductible. What this means is when you invest money in a retirement account, the amount invested is deducted from the level of income on which you need to pay taxes. This dynamic adds value in two ways. First, you pay less in taxes, which means you have more net income—or income after taxes—to spend on other things, or save and invest in other areas. Second, your money grows faster as you have more to invest as it is not taxed. These two goals—sufficient earned net income and sufficient retirement investments—work beautifully together.

What you invest in and how it pays you once you are retired also has tax benefits that can be gained, to give another idea of managing taxes and income.

Now for the third goal—giving back. Donations to charity that can be tracked, also known as philanthropy, are tax deductible. This means when you donate money to a charity, the amount of money you donate is deducted from the level of income on which you need to pay taxes. So the goal of giving back works in concert with the goal of having sufficient earned net income.

What is clear from this example is the need to think about your goals in life, lay them out, and see how they fit together when it comes to money management. Again, this is not something that you have to do alone. You can work with experts like accountants, lawyers, financial planners, and investment advisers. We will discuss what types of experts you might need, and how best to work with them, in Chapter 10. However, what you can think about now is the holistic picture of your wealth and how you want to live your life. Surprisingly, understanding and properly managing something that might seem dry or scary or negative like taxes can be an effective and empowering way to fulfill your dreams.

The Logistics

Paying and managing taxes is something that girls and young women in high school and college may not have a lot of experience with, so it is important that they understand the logistics. The logistics of income tax is a good place to start. The first step is for young people to understand that when they receive a paycheck, it will only be for a percentage of the "gross" or total salary that they are being paid. They also need to understand that they may pay taxes at the federal, or national, state, or local level. The higher the state and local taxes are, the more money they will pay in taxes in addition to the federal taxes. Some states do not have a state income tax, which is something some people take into account when deciding where to live.

On the federal level, the percentage paid in taxes, or the "tax bracket" a tax payer is in, will vary with their income. With a first job out of college, it is likely the salary is low enough that the young person will likely be in one of the lower federal tax brackets. The most common way to pay taxes with a salaried job is for the taxes to be withheld from the paycheck each time it is paid. Usually the amount withheld is more of an estimate of what the person expects she will owe in taxes at the end of the year, based on her life situation, like if she is single or married, or has children, and other factors.

During the year, it is a very good idea to keep track of different potential deductions, like charitable contributions, unreimbursed work expenses,
moving expenses, and other expenditures that are legal deductions that
year. Having a file folder to store receipts is an excellent way to keep physical records of potential tax deductions. It also makes sense to talk to an
accountant as soon as a first job starts, so that planning can be done
throughout the year ahead of tax time. An accountant can also help you
estimate how much tax you need to have withheld from each paycheck.

The tax year for individuals is the calendar year, so you pay taxes on the
year from January 1 to December 31. After the year ends, you have until
April 15 to complete your tax forms and submit them to the government,
including federal and possibly state, that require them. An accountant can
help you complete the forms. If you had more tax withheld from your paycheck than you ended up owing for the year based on the calculations on
your tax form, then you will get a refund from the government after you
file your tax forms. If you did not have enough tax withheld based on the
calculations of your tax return, you will need to send in a payment with
your tax returns to make up that difference when you file your taxes.

Do Try This at Home!

Giving back, or philanthropy, is not only a great value to teach our
children but also an effective tax planning and wealth management tool.
Research also shows that although not all young people are interested in
learning about money, many are interested in changing the world by helping those less fortunate. So philanthropy can also be a wonderful tool of
financial engagement.

This exercise involves the discovery part of philanthropy—meaning,
articulating your values and finding causes that support them. It also
involves the element of bringing people together to help work for the greater
good, a dynamic that is connected to social entrepreneurship, which we
will discuss further in Chapter 11.

Here is how the exercise works:

- Take some time to think about what matters to you, in terms of what your
  values are, and what you think is important.
- Research charities that align with those values. For example, if you love animals and abhor the mistreatment of animals, you can research charities like
  The Humane Society.
- Figure out if you would like to give a little money to many charities or a lot
  of money to one or a few charities.

- Think of how you might work together with your friends to achieve even more for the charity.
- Come up with a philanthropy plan for donating to one or more charities aligned with your values.

Discussion Points

Here are some additional discussion points you can share with the young woman in your life about how to think about taxes as part of an overall successful wealth planning program. Financial conversations using these discussion points can be had whenever is convenient—at breakfast, in the car, during family time, or a specially prescribed time to talk about money in a group or a club.

1. *Why do we pay taxes?* Income taxes are levied by the government to pay for public goods, like roads, bridges, parks, police, and other kinds of defense. Other taxes exist too, like sales tax and property tax.
2. *How is income tax determined?* Income taxes are based on a percentage of your earnings, minus certain things that are exempt and can be subtracted from your income, known as deductions. Generally, the more money you earn, the more tax you pay.
3. *Paying income taxes.* Income taxes can be taken directly out of a paycheck, or you can pay taxes owed for the previous year on April 15, which is tax day in the United States. Either way, income taxes mean that the salary you actually take home is lower than the salary you are offered by an employer.

How to Make a Difference with Philanthropy

1. Think about what matters to you and how you might want to change the world for the better.
2. Research nonprofit organizations that do the kind of work that interests you.
3. Put together a plan for donating money to these charities, possibly by working with friends with the same interests.

CHAPTER NINE

Insurance: The Ultimate Hedge

Introduction

Risk is as inevitable as . . . death and taxes.

And just like taxes, understanding and managing risk—although it may not seem glamorous—is critical to being financially literate, managing wealth, and being financially successful. Risk factors into so many areas of your financial life, and becoming comfortable with it and all of the ways it can be mitigated, can provide great opportunity for financial success.

Yes, risk can be managed. First, let's look at what risk is so we can then figure out how to manage it. Risk is the chance that something can go wrong. It actually has a negative connotation. Many people view risk as the possibility that something may not go as expected, but in reality, it can be worse than that with the unexpected not having an upside. In a financial context, risk might mean that an investment loses value instead of gains value, for a stock or a bond, or even a house you bought. Other forms of risk that can impact a financial picture are possibilities like getting too sick to work and earn money, or having a car accident and having to replace your car, or having to pay to replace someone else's car or pay for their medical bills.

One way to protect yourself against financial risk is through insurance. Insurance is a great financial product because its cost is typically far less than its possible benefit. It can also provide peace of mind, which for some, there is no higher value. In this way, insurance is both a thing and a concept. Literal insurance is financial protection you can purchase for a price that protects your major assets—your home, your car, your health, your ability to earn income. Some of the most common types of insurance include:

- *House or apartment insurance.* Insurance that pays for the damage caused by theft, fire, storms, floods, and other natural disasters.
- *Auto insurance.* Insurance that pays for the damage from a car accident.
- *Health insurance.* Insurance that pays medical costs for everything from routine medical visits to major surgery.
- *Disability insurance.* Insurance that replaces all or part of a person's income in the event she or he can't work due to an illness or injury.
- *Long-term care insurance.* Insurance that provides for the costs of long-term care for the elderly beyond any other benefits they might have.
- *Life insurance.* Insurance that pays a sum of money to a person's benefactors when the person dies.

The way insurance works is that a group of people pay what is known as a premium for the insurance, meaning an amount each year, to the insurance company. In turn, if the insured people need to use the insurance, the insurance company pays what it has promised contractually to pay in that situation. For example, if you have auto insurance and you have a car accident and need to have your car repaired, the insurance company will pay for the repair, minus any costs you have agreed contractually to pay. However, the way insurance works is that you may pay a premium for auto insurance every year you own your car, even if you never have a need for the insurance company to pay for anything. The premiums that all insured customers pay are pooled by the insurance company, and from that pool, payments are paid out as needed. The insurance keeps the excess premiums as revenue.

Insurance is a critical part of any financial plan because it protects against a worst-case scenario, meaning, a cost so great that you may not be able to afford to pay it, or if you do pay it, you will be in a financially challenging situation now and possibly for years to come. But insurance also has a cost—this protection does not come for free. So part of the analysis of buying insurance, including which type of insurance and for how much coverage, is quantifying the risk involved in the situation that you are insuring, and the value that the insurance provides, to make sure the cost is appropriate.

By the same token, risk is analyzed by the insurance company selling the policy. In the analysis of the insurance company, or seller, the more likely the insurance will be used, the more the policy will cost the buyer.

The insurance company makes more money if it pays out less for insurance, so a buyer who is more likely to use the insurance is considered a higher risk, so that buyer will have to pay more for the protection the insurance offers. For example, a person who has had an auto accident will pay more for car insurance than a person who has not, because people who have had an auto accident are viewed to be at greater risk of having another one.

Insurance as a form of risk management is an important concept for girls and young women to learn in finance. Insurance can mean protection in any scenario, as in a financial hedge in the markets, or a backup plan for a career move, like having a bridge job to pay the bills while you are starting your own business. Insurance really just means a protection against loss. Women need to be especially sensitive to issues in pricing with long-term care insurance, given that they live longer, and gender-distinct pricing can mean they pay much more than men.

Insurance comes for a cost, whether or not you ever need to use it. So part of the insurance analysis is deciding what kind of insurance you need, and another part of the insurance analysis is determining how much you should pay for it so that it has value.

As we know, insurance is protection—a hedge against the worst-case scenario. But there's a way to value it, and girls need to grasp this so that they can act in their own best interests. Understanding risk and how to value it is a huge part of being financially literate, and successful, and a critical part of an overall wealth management program. Managing risk is all about having the right insurance, careful tax planning, investing for different life phases and priorities, and having savings and other financial cushions in place for unexpected financial and family difficulties. Confidence comes from having a plan, but it also comes from knowing there are protections in place.

Financial Nutrition® Method: Protection Is (Almost) All Things

- Money as commodity
- *Risk*
- *Value*
- *Opportunity costs*
- *Information*

Insurance, when it comes to financial management, is truly a many splendored thing. It is a critical part of any wealth management plan because it protects assets and financial stability by helping to manage risk in an uncertain world. The right kind of insurance could well be one of the most important components of your financial life.

First and foremost, insurance manages *risk*. Risk, or the possibility that something can go wrong, plays a big part in financial stability. Insurance helps mitigate risk, meaning, it can make financial stability more likely. Risk has another role with insurance, and the cost of insurance, which is that as the price of insurance goes up the more likely it will be used by the insured, or the "riskier" the insured person is. So, the risk analysis is being done on both sides—by the insurance seller and the insurance buyer.

Value is also a part of the insurance equation. In the analysis of what kind of insurance to get, and how much to spend on it, an understanding of the value it provides is vital.

Opportunity costs come into play because the money spent on insurance that may or may not actually be utilized, depending on the life events that occur, is money that could be spent elsewhere. However, there could similarly be an opportunity cost to not having insurance—the opportunity cost of not having to spend money on a financial risk that could have been avoided if you did own insurance.

Finally, *information* is a very important part of the insurance analysis, especially in the quantification of risk. In order to analyze how risky something is, and how much it could cost in a worst-case scenario, information is necessary. Additionally, information is necessary to understand different kinds of insurance plans, their costs, and their value.

Insurance in the Context of Risk

When I talk to my students about insurance, they initially have more of an understanding of the abstract idea than the actual product. They may have an understanding that their family has health insurance because they have seen their insurance card when they go to the doctor's office, or that their mother has auto insurance because they have been involved in an auto accident. But as in the case of much of adult-life financial management, they do not have much of an understanding of the logistics of insurance, as they have not needed to.

The great thing is that it is possible to engage and connect with girls around the more abstract idea of insurance, or the need for protection or a backup. They also understand risk and the potential for things to go very badly. They have learned in other financial areas, like borrowing and investing, that risk has a cost. So teaching about insurance is a brilliant opportunity to put all of those important issues together and to make them all understandable in a financial analysis.

It is an interesting connection to make with the cost of risk in the context of insurance, after students have learned about the cost of risk in other contexts, like the interest charged on a loan, or the risk relationship to the return on an investment. In each of these cases, risk can be quantified in terms of a cost—or a benefit—to the consumer.

With insurance, the risk is a probability, or the potential that something bad could happen, and greater financial resources will be needed to take care of the situation. Examples of these things are illness, car wrecks, home thefts or fires, and death. Although this is a pretty negative list, the reality is, bad things do happen, but the impact can be lessened if financial resources, like insurance, are available to help manage the crisis. That is a huge value to insurance, of course. Some people even feel that insurance provides peace of mind, because worry is lessened regarding what will happen in times of crisis. That peace of mind, to some people, has tremendous value.

Looking at the other financial contexts of risk in comparison, the cost of risk can be viewed in terms of a borrower's creditworthiness or likelihood to repay a loan according to the terms originally agreed to. The lower a borrower's creditworthiness, the riskier the lender views the borrower to be, and so the interest rate or cost of money of the loan, goes up. In other words, risky borrowers pay higher interest rates for loans.

When it comes to investing, the higher the risk, the higher the potential return. So, in other words, an investor is sometimes "paid" more (in terms of potential return) for taking greater risk. This risk can be demonstrated in the form of investment price volatility, which means that the price moves up and down a lot. That price movement is risky because it is seen to be unpredictable, but at the same time it offers investors the opportunities to both buy low and sell high. But of course, there is risk involved!

So students can learn how to understand and quantify risk through credit, investing, and insurance. These areas are all pieces of the financial puzzle, and risk in those financial settings operates similarly. Students can come to realize that understanding and managing risk in all areas of their financial life will promote financial stability and even success.

Women and Risk

Risk and insurance are important topics for women, given trends in earning, investing, growing financial responsibility for their families, and life span. As we discussed in Chapter 7, women can be more risk-averse than men, which can hurt them in the area of investing and saving enough for retirement, as women do not always invest enough in the higher-risk assets like stocks, that they need earlier in life, in order to build sufficient wealth for retirement.[1] Risk aversion can be viewed as more of a positive in the insurance space but still needs to be managed financially.

Research shows that women's risk aversion can be a result of the issues around the gender wage gap and having less access to capital.[2] What this means is that because women earn less, they are not as open to taking financial risks. In the case of things going badly, like losing a lot of money in an investment, women who earn 78 percent of what men earn for full-time work have less opportunity to recoup their losses. Women also move in and out of the workforce more frequently, so they do not save as much over a lifetime compared to men.[3]

This lower access to capital means that women face certain barriers to engaging in responsible financial behaviors. Specifically, they may not feel comfortable taking risks in investing because they have less money to lose, and it is harder for them to make it back. In that context, risk aversion makes sense. This is a different case than if women had sufficient capital and were choosing not to invest it wisely. However, the combination of the lower earnings and risk-averse investing style mean can have negative consequences in retirement.

Let's step back and take a broader look at women and risk now that there are so many competing contexts, both positive and negative. The characteristics of women and money include a lot of strikes against—aversion to risk, lower wages, and recent trends are showing as well that women are taking more financial responsibility in families, as well as entering the workforce in greater numbers. Women also outlive men so need more years of retirement savings, but as the research shows, are almost twice as likely as men to end their lives below the poverty line.[4]

Women are increasingly becoming the primary wage earners in households with children, which means care and economic responsibility for children as well as adults.[5] In some cases, women are the sole wage earners in these families—an even greater financial burden, and responsibility. Insurance in these situations of more responsibility and lower earnings is critical. Property, health, and auto insurance for the basic costs that can impact any family are extremely important. But any adult who has an income that is needed in a family needs to consider long-term disability insurance, which typically covers a percentage of a salary if you become disabled and unable to work. Life insurance is also important, as it can replace the income if a primary breadwinner in a family passes away, but the income is still needed.

Although death is not most people's favorite topic, in the context of financial management, it is an important life event to consider. There is the case for life insurance to replace the income of the primary breadwinners, but there is also the need for insurance for the costs of a longer life.

As women tend to outlive men, and save less for retirement, long-term care insurance is a very important need. Long-term care insurance covers the costs of care for the elderly, costs that are only increasing with time.

These same issues of lower earnings and less savings over a lifetime and for retirement are specific reasons why certain types of insurance are really important for women. In general, the less money you have saved for emergencies or to pay for costs like doctor's visits, the more you are going to need to rely on insurance to cover those costs. So, property, health, and auto insurance should be utilized effectively in financial management, with families, single women, and in all stages of life.

Insurance Basics: What Kind, How Much, and When?

So it's clear that insurance is an important part of a financial plan and that women have specific needs and priorities. Another important consideration is the analysis that goes into the types of insurance needed within the broad categories already discussed, how much and what type of coverage is needed, and when to buy it. This analysis is truly a risk analysis for both the insurance buyer and the insurance seller—quantifying the potential cost of the damage that can be done if the worst thing happens, and the percent chance that it will actually happen. The other analysis is the value question—how much should you pay for insurance to maximize the value of the protection.

Let's look at the second question first. The cost of insurance varies from provider to provider, just like any other product, so it is important to shop around and compare costs. The cost also varies as to how much and what kind of insurance is needed, as well as the likelihood the insurance will actually be paid out. The latter analysis is done by the insurance company, or seller of the insurance, while the other analyses are done by the consumer, or buyer of the insurance.

But the comparison needs to be consistent, meaning, you need to compare the same kind of coverage versus the same kind of coverage. First of all, the same type of insurance needs to be compared, for example, life insurance policies versus each other or auto insurance policies versus each other. Then, within the same type of policy, you need to compare the same quality of coverage.

Individual costs that contribute to the overall cost of coverage include the deductible, and the amount of insurance coverage that can be paid out if the insurance needs to be utilized. A deductible is the portion that the consumer pays when the insurance is used. For example, with auto insurance, if a car accident happens and the insurance payout is needed to pay to repair the car, the consumer might pay a small share, known as the deductible. The deductible is an amount that is set at the time the policy is purchased. For example, the deductible might be $250 or $500. The difference in these amounts can mean a significant difference in the overall cost of the policy.

The amount of insurance coverage can also vary. For example, if you are comparing life insurance policies, you would want to compare two policies that pay $1 million each at the time of death, rather than one policy that pays $1 million and one that pays $500,000. Typically, a $1 million policy will cost more in annual premiums than a $500,000 policy because of the difference in what the insurance company will have to pay if the policy is paid out.

Interestingly, risk comes into play as well when insurance providers price the insurance. For example, the more likely it is that you will use the insurance, the more expensive it will be to you. This is because when the insurance company has to pay out a claim for an insurance holder, it is a cost to the company, and viewed therefore as a risk. So the riskier you are as an insured person, the more you will likely have to pay for that insurance.

A few examples of this risk-cost correlation include auto insurance and life insurance. Auto insurance costs increase when you have auto accidents. This is because insurance companies have done an analysis that shows that people who have one accident are more likely to have another accident. Until you have your first auto accident, depending on your age, you may be viewed as a fairly low-risk driver. Insurance costs are similarly higher for younger drivers, as they are considered to be higher risks than older drivers, because younger drivers typically have less experience on the road and more accidents.

Life insurance also involves analyses around the likelihood of earlier life use. People who engage in behaviors that have been proven to be linked to disease and death, like smoking, will typically have to pay a higher cost for life insurance than people who have healthier living patterns. Similarly, the older you are, the more you will have to pay for life insurance as you are less likely to live as long as a younger person.

So one way to manage insurance costs is to try to have safe and healthy life habits and not be a high risk to insurers. This means being physically healthy if possible, maintaining your auto and driving carefully, and making sure your home is safe and secure. Of course, these things are not always possible, and even within the highest risk situations, it is important to do an analysis of the value of the insurance and the quantification of risk.

Risk quantification in an insurance context, from the perspective of the consumer or insurance buyer, means the likelihood you will need to use the insurance and how much value it has for you. Health insurance, for example, covers medical costs. In order to stay healthy, you need to go to the doctor regularly for different checkups and treatments at different points in your life. And of course there are medical costs that are not expected, which makes it difficult to anticipate what they will be and what they will cost.

The first analysis for health insurance, then, is the medical costs you are sure of like checkups and expected treatments, and if those costs are higher or lower than what you will have to pay for insurance. Then you can look at the costs of unexpected events like hospital stays, or outpatient treatments for illnesses you may not know you will have. Hospital stays and certain procedures are extremely expensive. It is more than likely that the cost of health insurance will not be as much as the cost of medical treatment that involves a hospital stay.

This analysis can be done for all types of insurance. Typically the analysis will show that of the major types of insurance discussed in this chapter, all are necessary. So the next analysis is to figure out how to get the best coverage—and appropriate coverage you need—for the best price. This is where cost comparisons come into play. As with any financial product, the costs will vary as to the company, and so will the service and individual attention. For example, you can work with a big insurance company where you do not receive a lot of individual attention, or you can work with an insurance broker who handles all of your needs and knows you personally. It is likely, though, that any kind of insurance that comes with a high level of personalized service will cost more because the company's costs are higher.

Experts can also help with this analysis, and given the importance of insurance to your long-term health and well-being, and your financial picture, talking to the right expert can make a lot of sense. Insurance of all different types can also be complicated, with different options at different costs. Then in addition, there is the analysis of what you can afford and what you need to be able to afford. Finally, there is the quantification of risk—understanding what is the likelihood that you may need different types of insurance.

It's important to understand risk, and insurance, so that you can trust your instinct when it comes to protecting your wealth, and potentially, your family. As we discussed in Chapter 7 on investing, you do not have to be an expert. We all have our areas of expertise, and you don't have to be an expert in all things. Any area, where a significant amount of money and some expertise are involved, warrants considering working with an expert. When you do look for an expert, find one who provides what you need—a style that is comfortable for you and all the information you want. This relationship is a very important one, so make sure you feel good about it, and don't hire someone until you do. We will be discussing finding the right experts more in Chapter 10.

Hedging

Hedging is a fantastic tool in the financial markets for protecting against investment risk to the downside. It can be complicated and require quantitative skills, as well as insight into a diverse array of markets. "Hedging your bets" is an expression that reflects the financial meaning of the term. But hedging means something else too.

Hedging can also mean protection in any form. Sometimes hedging has a negative connotation, like not making a commitment to one thing or another, or at least, playing two sides of something.

Teenagers have the ability to understand hedging as well as adults do. Teenagers are facing higher stakes and more stress earlier on, with more academic pressure and competitive college admissions, student loans and the demand for a certain level of salary after college, and being generally forced to make choices about their future at a much earlier age.

So understanding the ability to protect yourself in an uncertain world, or at least to recognize different options and paths, is critical for young people, particularly young women. The students in my classes recognize that they have the potential for many different life paths, big careers or more simple ones, motherhood, entrepreneurship, some combination of some or all of the above. Along with this understanding of options—which of course can carry with it its own kind of stress—understanding the idea of hedging, or insurance, can help them take measured risks in exploring different life options. With the right approach to this type of exploration, they can be protected if one of the life paths does not work out exactly as planned.

A great example of this is entrepreneurship, which we will explore more in Chapter 11. Starting your own business or nonprofit is becoming an increasingly viable way to make a living and have an interesting and fulfilling life. Many women are drawn to entrepreneurship because of the lack of a glass ceiling for salary or position. However, entrepreneurship comes with its fair share of risks, first and foremost, economic inconsistency. It can be tough to establish consistent, sufficient revenue and cash flow right off the bat with a new venture, and sometimes not ever.

However, there are certainly options for insurance, or hedging, when starting a new enterprise. One way is to have another job at the same time, known as a bridge job, that provides sufficient income, while starting up a new venture. Certainly this could mean a very busy life, but it also insures adequate income while the new venture is in its early, unstable years. It is also a good idea, if the new venture ever becomes a full-time job, to maintain networks for a career that may be interesting—or necessary—in the future. This is another form of hedging.

Do Try This at Home!

Insurance in a financial program is all about protecting against, and quantifying, risk. This exercise focuses on helping girls understand how risk is present in their lives, and what they can do to manage it, as a foundation for learning about insurance.

Here is how the exercise works:

- Think about what risk means to you, and where you see it in your life. Write down three risks in your life that you are concerned about. They can be anything from a type of financial concern, to grades or assignments due at school, or things in your personal life.
- Then, brainstorm different ways you protect against that risk. For example, if you feel like there is a risk of doing badly in a class that is hard or you are struggling in, think about what you might do to help minimize that risk. Some ideas might be asking the teacher for help, setting aside more time to study, or asking more questions in class.
- Write down three different alternative plans you can put in place to protect against that risk. Then, write down three different plans for each of the other two risks.
- Finally, think about how you can live a life where there is less risk. See if you can find any trends in the types of risks you wrote down and in the ideas and plans you had for insuring against the risks.

Discussion Points

1. *Insurance is both a concept and a literal thing.* Insurance as a concept is a protection against something bad happening, including having a backup plan for a school project or career path. Insurance makes sense in all areas of life, including your financial life. When it comes to your financial life, although insurance has a cost, it can save you money in the long run and help protect your financial well-being. In other words, actual insurance is a financial product you can purchase that protects your health, home, auto, and other things.

2. *Risk can be quantified: Part 1.* In the same way that a lender will charge you higher interest for a loan if you are a risky borrower, meaning less likely to repay the loan, insurance plans will cost more if you are viewed to be a risk for that type of insurance. For example, if you engage in unhealthy behaviors or have a lot of auto accidents, your insurance costs in those areas might be higher.

3. *Risk can be quantified: Part 2.* Risk can also be measured by the consumer, or the buyer of the insurance. Given your personal situation, you can analyze how likely it is that certain things might happen in your life that you need to insure against. For example, if you have a young child, you know there is a likelihood that you will need to go to the doctor a lot because young children are more prone to illness.

4. *Insurance is a part of an effective financial plan.* Insurance can help protect you against major financial losses, like a house fire or theft, a major car accident, or a terrible illness. All of these events are frequently unexpected but cost a lot of money. So it is important to be sure to plan adequately for the possibility, so you don't take a major financial hit if any of them occur, and so you can get the best care you need for yourself, your house, and your auto.

HOW TO MANAGE RISK

1. Brainstorm the risk you have in your life.
2. Come up with different plans to protect against the risk.
3. Think of how you can live a life with less risk.

CHAPTER TEN

Financial Information Sources: Education and Experts Matter

Introduction

We've talked a lot about how money can be scary. And happy, sad, shameful, generous, joyful, and empowering. But money is seldom rational—no matter how much we understand its potential—especially when we need it to be. Because money is emotional, and also part of big life decisions and financial security, pitfalls abound with psychology and behaviors around money and financial decision making. Both scary markets and exciting markets cause people to do silly and irrational things, like buy high and sell low. Similarly, buying or selling a home can also be fraught with emotions around family, security, life expectations, what could be, and what should be. So how can we teach girls to deal with the emotional side of money and effective financial decision making?

It may seem counterintuitive, but financial literacy also means knowing that it is not always possible to know how to make the best financial decision, or the best investment, despite a deep understanding of what is possible. Certainly financial education is a key part of the equation in gaining expertise and a disposition for the financial behaviors that can lead to financial independence and success. Financial literacy helps you know the right questions to ask when it comes to complicated and emotional financial transactions, and it also enables your instinct to speak loudly and confidently. It's important to know the market and understand the economy so that you can trust your instinct when it comes to investing. However, you do not have to be an expert.

Education about money can lead to healthier financial behaviors, which means learning how to make money work for you. Money does not have to be an uncontrollable force, waiting in the wings to wreak havoc because of something you did or did not do. Money does not have to be anything more than a tool to provide for oneself and one's family. It's that simple. But that control likely will not happen without understanding, and the sooner we start educating ourselves the better.

We all have our areas of expertise, and you don't have to be an expert in all things. But if you're not an investment expert, you may want to work with someone who is. When you do look for an expert, find one who provides what you need—a style that is comfortable for you and all the information you want. This relationship is a very important one, so make sure you feel good about it, and don't hire someone until you do.

Studies consistently show that women are underconfident about money. A lack of confidence can mute a willingness to listen to instinct. Helping young women build confidence with money and financial understanding is a critical piece of the puzzle. The more a young woman understands about money and finance, the sharper her instincts will be for making the right decisions about how to take care of herself financially, including choosing the right expert.

Why would you want to work with a financial expert, and when? Financial experts can add a great deal of value when it comes to managing money and life's big financial questions. A financial adviser, for example, can help you develop a financial plan for your life, which includes managing income, investing, tax and insurance planning, and estate planning and philanthropy. You can also hire specific experts in the areas of investing (also called financial or investment advisers), taxes (accountants), and estate planning (lawyers).

Research shows that women can be less interested in working with experts, like financial advisers, for a number of reasons. Among them is an interest in a certain type of relationship with the financial adviser. Women say that they don't like being talked down to and are instead looking for more of a collaborative partnership with an adviser. This concern is being addressed in the financial services industry, but for now, far fewer women than men work with financial advisers.

It is important when working with an expert that you find someone you trust and feel comfortable with. It can be a good idea to get a referral or a recommendation for the expert, either from someone you trust, or from a legitimate and well-regarded professional association related to the industry. The comfort level is important so that you ask questions, and feel free to disagree, or argue with different points and ideas if you do not agree with them.

Additionally, it is important to understand the cost—and value—associated with experts. They have varying costs and fees, but one important rule of thumb is their cost compared to the value they provide. For example, the value of a good accountant can come from the fact that she saves you more money by doing your taxes with her expertise, than if you did them yourself, that is an amount the same or higher than her cost. The other cost to consider, in addition to the monetary value of working with an expert, is time. If you are working with an expert, they will be taking care of things for you that you do not have to do yourself, freeing up time to work or do something else you enjoy.

Trusting your instinct when working with financial professionals is key to having effective, positive relationships with the experts who can help you be successful. This instinct can be honed by financial education, and open, frank conversations with the experts working on your behalf. Teaching girls to trust their instincts is a win-win no matter what but can also help in this important area.

So money can—and will—be scary, happy, and lots of other emotions depending on the circumstances. But understanding how to manage the consistently irrational aspect of money is what financial literacy is all about.

Financial Nutrition® Method: The Value of Information

- Money as commodity
- Risk
- *Value*
- Opportunity costs
- *Information*

Information is critical to financial management and has great *value*. Information is necessary on many levels—personal finance concepts like budgeting, saving, credit, and debt, for financial management, and more complex concepts for investing. Information can come in many forms—education, experts, and other resources. Education and engagement with your money in all areas is critical, including classes or self-education through books and media. Engagement means monitoring your money, the markets, and the economy, and staying in touch with a financial adviser if you have one. It is important to know what is happening in the world and how it is impacting your money and financial well-being.

You can also be educated and engaged by working with an expert, whether it is a financial or investment adviser, lawyer, accountant, or some other financial specialist. In the right relationship, education will be ongoing as you work together on helping to create the financial life that meets your goals. Experts also have value in a pure monetary sense, if the work they do on your taxes, or investments, or financial legal paperwork saves money or creates income that exceeds their cost. That is an important analysis though and should be part of a decision when to use an expert.

How Girls Handle Financial Information

Financial education has proven to be a popular, engaging topic for teenaged girls. When taught in New York City, my class was heavily subscribed as an afterschool or evening program, despite the students' busy schedules with schoolwork and college applications. The classes were not only full of students but also full of energy, and students explored financial areas that engaged them and helped them feel more empowered in their lives.

The classes tend to evolve as we move forward in the semester. My classes tend to include bright, well-educated, motivated young women, students who are used to getting the answer right. In fact, many of them really do not like to get the answer wrong, but finance tends to be an area where most teenagers do not have a lot of experience. The young women in my classes are ambitious, and bold, but yet when they first come to my class, they don't speak but prefer to listen. They stare at me from around the seminar table, cautious and uncertain, as I ask them basic questions about money.

I work hard to create a community in the classroom where students feel safe to get the answer wrong. Not only does it make a more comfortable and effective environment for learning but it also creates the possibility that the students know, for the rest of their lives, that it is okay to not understand finance, and it is even more okay to continually put themselves in a position to learn, and to get the answers they need to live a financially successful and secure life. It is okay to admit their lack of knowledge to an expert (in this case, their teacher) and to ask the right questions to develop their knowledge.

Before long, we have dynamic discussions, where students play with ideas, take risks, and begin to connect the dots on what they need to know and do to be financially literate and successful. This scenario plays out in class, after class, after class. This interesting and compelling dynamic that occurs in the financial education classroom is one I like to call the development of confidence through information.

The acquisition of a deeper knowledge comes through learning from me, an expert, from our readings, from engaging fully in classroom activities, and from having the courage to make mistakes and learn from them. Through these actions, the young women in my classes develop confidence in themselves and in their ability to understand financial management. Slowly and consistently, the students come to a realization that the confidence they have in themselves when it comes to managing money will align with what they will be paid in the future, and the wealth they will build.

So the value of a good financial education program is many. First there is the knowledge acquisition of a critical area where a lot of learning opportunities do not typically present themselves in school or at home. With the knowledge, and the experiential activities and dialogue, can come an awareness and shift in disposition, and attitudes that lead to behavioral changes. One behavioral change for these young women that is as valuable as any other is the awareness and ability to ask questions and not feel like they have to know everything ahead of time.

This behavior, which is grounded in a confidence of sorts, is critical when working with an expert. Not only will asking questions help you continue to learn, but it makes you an active partner in the process. This is key given that no matter how good the expert is, it is your money, and your life, and you need to be sure that you have a sufficient understanding of your financial possibilities, and how to get there.

Self-Advocacy and Collaboration: How to Work with Experts

The theme here clearly is, you do not need to be an expert in all things, but you do need to find the right expert in critical financial areas of your life, if you are not going to be the expert. However, it is very, very important that you feel comfortable with the person and can have a learning, collaborative relationship with the expert. Their style, then, is important. You do not have to hire the first expert who comes along, and you are totally within your right to not hire anyone that does not suit you.

When you work with an expert, whether it's someone who manages money for you personally or manages a mutual fund that you invest in, there will be costs involved like commissions and expenses. These costs are how money managers get paid and earn a living. But these costs vary, and they should relate to the value the expert or fund is providing. So, if a manager or fund is expensive but their performance is not good, it's a lower-value proposition. Remember—you are not making money for yourself until your investment gains have covered the costs of that investment.

Research shows that women can be reticent about working with financial professionals. One recent study showed that only 35 percent of working women surveyed would trust financial professionals and accept their recommendations. According to the study, working women with higher financial literacy levels tend to trust financial professionals more than less financially literate. The issue is that women think financial professionals are too expensive and that it is hard to find the right financial professional for their personal situation.[1]

Other research shows that women have a variety of problems with the way they are treated in the financial services industry. Some studies show that women believe they are talked down to and frequently do not feel comfortable asking questions. Women would like to work in a collaborative environment, where they partner with the financial adviser. Women want to feel heard. Unfortunately, women do not always feel comfortable asking questions when they don't understand something, and don't always engage with their financial adviser, particularly when they have a male partner.

So what do women want? Women want to talk to a good listener about their hopes and dreams, fears and concerns, and goals for their family and their money. Women want to learn, and work in partnership, collaborating with their financial adviser as that person is taking control of what might be the most important part of their world—the care and upkeep of themselves and their families.[2]

Self-advocacy is critical too, especially if it is an area where women are classically less confident and less involved. Self-advocacy around money is critical, for all people. But for groups that face challenges to financial security and success in our still imperfect world, financial self-advocacy is an absolute necessity.

How do you find the right financial adviser? You can start with vetting professional advisers through industry organizations, understanding the fiduciary standard, and trusting your instincts.

Given women's unique financial challenges (like being systematically underpaid), we need financial education programs and financial advice services tailored to women. More and more financial firms are meeting this need, and self-advocacy in this area is both critical and complementary. So when we teach girls about learning to understand their worth, and articulate it, and ask for the salary they deserve, we are teaching them self-advocacy for their financial futures. In a perfect world, we would not have groups that are discriminated against economically, but the world is not perfect.

In addition to self-advocating for income, taking responsibility for one's financial future—with the help of experts when needed—is another form of self-advocacy. Financial education is not systematic in the United States and may not be for a long time, or possibly ever. So while we wait for a perfect world to come around in the area of financial education, women and girls need to learn to take responsibility for the knowledge and advice they need to succeed financially. Working with professionals in a collaborative relationship where ongoing education is a key component is one way to get there.

Education = Engagement = Confidence

Education and engagement with your money in all areas is critical. For investing, it is important to make sure you educate yourself on an ongoing basis, including self-education through books and media, or formal education through classes, or working closely with an expert. Engagement means monitoring your money, the markets, and the economy, and staying in touch with your financial adviser if you have one. It's important to understand what is happening in the world and how it is impacting your money.

Study after study shows that men tend to be more confident than women when it comes to investing. To be clear, that male confidence is not always aligned completely with competence and success in the markets. Even so, the underconfidence some women exhibit with investing can be particularly damaging to their wealth creation. The issue is that it leads to underinvestment in risky assets needed to provide the level of return necessary to create wealth for a secure retirement, and other needs.

The best way to deal with a lack of confidence for women of all ages— this can start as young as a teen and go through to those who are retired— is to self-educate, stay current with the markets, and work with professionals who collaborate in that process. Knowledge is power, as we know, and understanding how markets work, what is going on in the economy today, and speaking with experts who are themselves knowledgeable and confident enough to be collaborative in the investing process, is the key to greater confidence. That greater knowledge and confidence should lead, hopefully in short order, to higher returns on investments and healthy wealth development.

It is important to learn the basics of investing and markets and how the economy works. Believe me, it's easier than it may sound. But you can't really know the specifics well without understanding the big picture. Take a class or two, read high-quality books, or seek out possibilities online, including webinars, and other web-based instruction. Find something that fits your schedule and stick with it. Make sure your girls are being educated about money from a young age. Starting young will help create a stronger foundation of confidence and understanding.

Additionally, on an ongoing basis, it is important to read high-quality financial publications. This could be newspapers or websites, on a daily basis, that engage high-quality journalism to explain what is happening around the globe, and how those occurrences in turn impact markets, and eventually, your financial security. You need to understand what is happening in the world, and in the markets, and how it is impacting your money now and over time.

You can engage by starting to put your money to work. For the younger set, this means working with parents to invest small amounts of money, or learning more about the money that has already been invested on their behalf. For the over-21 crowd, start with a retirement plan. Know if you have one through your job, know what's in it, and follow a strategy that is appropriate for your age and saving goals. Follow it on a quarterly basis, and rebalance it every year based on your investing strategy and long-term goals.

And of course, if that last part about investing, strategy, and goals sounds daunting, or if you are interested in doing investing in addition to your retirement plan, try working with an expert. As we have discussed in this book we all have our areas of expertise, and you don't have to be an expert in all things. When you look for an expert to help you with investing and wealth management, make sure you find one who helps with your learning process and collaborates with you in the process. This person can coach you and be a partner in the development of your confidence.

What the Development of Money Confidence Looks Like

In a recent program for girls in New York City, in our first class we discussed the context of women and money, looking at issues around the gender wage gap, women and work, girls' rising ambition levels, and the importance of income in the overall financial picture. We did our fantastic exercise on salary negotiations, so the girls could begin to understand—and experience—that critical process.

When we came back together for a debrief of the activity, the girls discussed the challenges of the process and also the exultation when they had made a strong argument for a raise in the simulation, and gotten it. We talked about what it would take for them to negotiate a higher salary in a real-life situation. I am always impressed with the realizations the salary negotiation exercise provides. In the exercise, as we discussed in Chapter 3, the girls have to make a case for why they should be paid more.

During the debrief discussion, one student remarked that she could see how much confidence in herself would align with what she would be paid in the future. This is a life-changing realization, in both a personal sense, and in financial potential. Without confidence in your own worth, it can be difficult, or even impossible, to make a cogent argument on your own behalf or even start the conversation for a higher salary. Asking for a raise, or negotiating a higher starting salary than was originally offered, is a form of risk, particularly for women. But in dealing with risk in both investing and salary negotiations, confidence is critical.

Money confidence is about believing in your ability to take care of yourself financially and involves the ongoing learning and demonstration of the skills, mindset, and deeper understanding of how the critical financial pieces of your life fit together. These pieces include human capital, wealth management, and value creation.

The "what" of money confidence might seem complicated, although I believe with the right education, it is well within everyone's grasp. The "why" is simple but powerful. Money confidence matters because its manifestation is the basis for financial health and success.

Do Try This at Home!

Learning how to work with financial experts is important. One way to build a foundation in working with experts is to consider the experts in your life and how you could learn more from them, and self-advocate as well as collaborate in the relationship.

Here is how the exercise works: Think of the experts in your life. They could be teachers, doctors or other medical professionals, coaches, and even your parents.

- Choose one expert in an area of your life where you would like to grow and develop further.
- Brainstorm ideas of how you might collaborate more with the expert in that area of your life, so that you can learn more and improve yourself in that area.
- Write down a list of these methods, and try to utilize them to collaborate more effectively with, and learn more from, your expert.

Discussion Points

Here are some discussion points you can share with the young woman in your life about how to financially self-educate. Financial conversations using these discussion points can be had whenever is convenient—at breakfast, in the car, during family time, or a specially prescribed time to talk about money in a group or a club.

1. *Read the paper.* You may already be doing this, and kudos to you if so. But if not, make a point of reading the major news every day,

including at least one article about the stock market. Choose a well-regarded newspaper or website like *The New York Times, The Wall Street Journal,* or Bloomberg.com. What happens in the world impacts your money, to put it simply, and following the story on a daily basis will help you begin to make the connections you need to for understanding the bigger picture of your financial health.

2. *Take a class.* A class does not have to take over your life. You can find something local and easy to attend or something online that fits your schedule any time of the day or night. The beauty of a class is it's a commitment, it's structured, and it will have standards. It can be difficult to make time to learn about money even though it is so important, and a class will require you to carve out that space in your life, for a potential big gain.

3. *Talk about money.* This one falls into the category for many parents, of being willing to do things for your kids that you do not take time to do for yourself. Talking to your kids about money is a double bonus. It features the obvious positive of teaching kids about money at a young age, so that they can grow up to be financially knowledgeable and healthy adults. But the extra advantage is that it will encourage you to learn more about money, even just by articulating what you already know.

4. *Start investing.* Again, you may already be doing this, and if so, that's great. If not, the beauty of investing is it is a way to help earn the money you need for retirement, and it is an experiential approach to learning about money. I do not recommend throwing a bunch of money into the stock market with complete abandon. Start with step 1 and step 2, or skip right to working with an expert who you trust, feel comfortable with, and who can collaborate with you in the process so that you both learn to understand investing, and enjoy it.

WORKING WITH EXPERTS

1. Think of an expert in your life, a relationship in which you would like to grow and learn more.
2. Write down different ways you could work more effectively with that person.
3. Try to utilize those ways to work more effectively with your expert.

CHAPTER ELEVEN

Entrepreneurship: Think in a New Way

Entrepreneurship is extraordinary for many reasons. Frequently, new ventures—whether commercial or socially focused—are created to solve a problem, provide a better solution, or approach something completely differently. So the venture creation can be a creative, smart, and meaning-ful act that helps a lot of people, or makes people's lives better, or moves an industry forward. In other words, entrepreneurial ventures can provide products and services that make our lives better, more enjoyable, or easier. They can provide answers and solutions to widespread social problems like disease, hunger, or resource shortages. Entrepreneurship brings life, form, and function—and maybe even income—to new ideas.

So that means that entrepreneurs are special people, who frequently get to think in different ways and develop a skill set that helps them not only in business but in life. That is one of the many positives of entrepreneur-ship. Because of the need to deal with failure in the many phases of starting a new venture, certain skills need to be developed and strengthened, like creativity, resilience, risk analysis, tenacity, communication, and financial skills. These are strengths that are important in business and in life.

Another area entrepreneurship addresses is the need to self-actualize, in a very public way. This means, in part, valuing who you are and what you have created and actually telling people about it and trying to get them to support you in different ways. Although the entrepreneur has the idea and guides the ship, even one with resources needs to rely on others for support, whether it be investment or other funding, networking, technical expertise in different areas, or plain and simple emotional support through the stressful times. Being an entrepreneur can mean giving credit to others and working with a team, but it also means putting yourself out there and letting the world hear about *your* great ideas.

Entrepreneurship can be appealing to women for lots of reasons. First off, there is that stubborn gender wage gap that means women earn less than their potential, not to mention the "glass ceiling" that—in whatever form it takes—can mean that women rise less frequently to high positions. Well, the beauty of owning your own company, is there is no one there to pay you too little, or keep you from ascending to the highest post in the company. Of course, starting and running a successful business is no mean feat (to say the least!). But if it works, it can provide so many things, including possibly even flexibility for those who may want to pursue more than one career, or additional education, or have a family, as well as a job or career.

Entrepreneurship fits really well into a financial literacy program for girls and not just because women are trending more in that direction. Entrepreneurship learning can be a very impactful part of financial education. One of the challenges of teaching about money to younger folks who may not yet have any real financial responsibility is the experiential component. Understanding money is often a learning-by-doing enterprise, so ideas like compound interest, mortgages, and investing can be alien to the younger set who have not yet engaged with those concepts in a real-world context.

Although students do express interest in these ideas, as well as in budgeting, spending, saving, and other important financial concepts and behaviors, full-on engagement can be an issue if the material is presented only theoretically. Teaching about starting a business, and the financial processes that go into it, can provide an exciting context for learning about how money works. This holds attention and solidifies understanding.

Interestingly, though, I am finding that more and more young women are actually interested in starting their own enterprise, whether for-profit or socially based. I can understand this interest from the context of women and money. The women entrepreneurs I know are motivated by income potential and time flexibility, being their own boss and not having to worry about discriminatory barriers, and usually, a sincere interest in serving others and making life better. For some women, having their own business is the most effective way to overcome income inequality, bypass discriminatory barriers, and find a way to do fulfilling, meaningful work on their own terms.

As an educator, I see huge value in teaching girls and young women about entrepreneurship, whether or not they want to own their own business one day. Entrepreneurship is all about creativity and resourcefulness. Equally important are the required elements of tenacity and resiliency—every entrepreneur knows in their world, it is a must to embrace failure and to learn to bounce back with an even better idea. Entrepreneurship demands a certain amount of fearlessness and measured risk taking, which can be translated more positively into self-confidence and belief in one's abilities. Idea generation and opportunity recognition are also key to starting a new venture.

Whether the venture is for-profit or socially minded, entrepreneurship is all about finding a better way, a new way, or maybe even the only way, to help make life better. And the amazing thing is, in addition to being an opportunity to create a business or social venture that might even change the world, it provides the opportunity, and in many cases demands, that the entrepreneur becomes the best person she can be.

Entrepreneurship Is Financial Nutrition®!

- *Money as a commodity*
- *Risk*
- *Value*
- *Opportunity costs*
- *Information*

Entrepreneurship encompasses all of the areas of the Financial Nutrition® Method, as it is financial management plain and simple, but for a business or nonprofit organization rather than an individual. However, there are many overlaps between the financial knowledge and skills needed to run a business and run a personal life, like cash flow, budgeting, credit, debt, and having goals. It is a great context for girls and young women to learn about money management for that reason, as it is engaging and all-encompassing of financial topics, but entrepreneurship can be fun and creative too.

In the context of entrepreneurship, to put it simply, *money as a commodity*, in the forms of cash flow and revenue and expenditures, as well as funding and external investment, is critical to managing an enterprise, whether for-profit or nonprofit. Money is a necessary and primary fuel to get the venture going, and succeeding. *Risk* is very real in starting a new venture, because nobody knows if it will be successful or not. Launching your own business or organization in some ways can be a huge gamble. Of course, as with all risk, there are ways to manage it. But risk in entrepreneurship is also very financial, as the start-up costs for a company are an investment, and the return could be positive—the company is successful, or negative—the company is not successful, or even completely fails. In the case of failure, large amounts of money that were put into the venture to get it started could be completely lost.

Value plays a role in all kinds of analysis in the company, including determining what markets to go into, or articulating a value proposition to funders, investors, or potential consumers. *Opportunity costs*—weighing different options of where to spend resources—is a constant and ongoing process in a start-up. And finally, *information* is critical for so many different reasons and might be the most important resource in the rapidly changing environment of a start-up.

Entrepreneurship Interest Is on the Rise

The first day of my financial education classes are usually filled with energy, as the girls who are taking the class do not really know what to expect. They are girls with ambition and a thirst for financial knowledge, certainly, or they would not be taking the time out of their busy lives to take the class. These are girls who are not used to not knowing the answer—they work hard, study, and come to class prepared. But in my class, they do not even know the questions yet. So they are excited but anxious. I try to break the ice with getting to know them. One way I do it is by asking them what they want to be when the grow up.

On the first day of one of my classes, when the students from a high school class in New York City were asked if they wanted to be entrepreneurs, 17 of the 19 girls raised their hands. That's 90 percent. I was pretty astounded! But also pleased and very impressed. And while this interest in being an entrepreneur is an interesting trend and worth investigating, I was even more excited about how learning about entrepreneurship now, while they are still in high school, could change these young women's lives.

So what happens when you teach young women about entrepreneurship? What do they learn, and what do they gain from the experience?

- *Experiential learning.* This means learning by doing. When learning about how to start a company, you have to work with real financial concepts and understand how money actually works, rather than just the *idea* of money, in the abstract.
- *Entrepreneurial thinking.* Learning to think like an entrepreneur is the crux of the matter and extremely valuable! It involves ultimately achieving innovative solutions by integrating creativity, vision, analytical reasoning, and

intellectual skills. You have to stretch your imagination, use your brain, ana-lyze an assortment of outcomes, and take measured risks, all at the same time.

- *Idea development.* Moving successfully through the multiple stages of idea development to venture creation requires the mobilization of interests and talents, as well as ambition and work ethic, all at the highest level. This intense effort leads to amazing projects and ventures for college portfolios and beyond.

- *Self-confidence.* A new and stronger sense of self, ability, and talent can be the result of creating something you never thought you could and learning you are capable of far more than you ever could have imagined.

Entrepreneurship education is nothing less than an incredibly power-ful way to help young women acquire knowledge, build confidence, embrace ambition, and be successful in all areas of life. Young women who are interested in becoming entrepreneurs should be encouraged—and educated—while they are still in high school because the experience could change their lives.

One great way to help young women learn to think like, and possibly become, entrepreneurs, is to have them create companies as a class proj-ect. These can be actual, or "model" ventures, either commercial or social. It can be especially beneficial to have the students work in teams, so they learn how to collaborate, and also how to leverage talents and skill sets across a small group. This exercise includes creating a business plan that delineates everything from the product description, competitive analysis, market research, and financial analysis. It is a powerful tool for financial understanding and personal development!

Trends Are Positive for Women Entrepreneurs

A recent study showed that daughters with mothers who were entre-preneurs had a "propensity" for it, meaning, the daughters were more likely to be self-employed if their mothers were. In fact, the heavy influ-ence of an entrepreneur mom actually negated the forces—like masculine stereotypes—that can act against women becoming entrepreneurs.[1]

According to the U.S. Census, women-owned businesses are 36 percent of all firms.[2] This increase is in line with greater numbers of women in the labor force, and more women acting as the primary breadwinners in their families. So entrepreneurship—or owning your own business—is becoming an increasingly viable option for women as they continue to expand into the workforce and into familial financial responsibility.

Babson University does a biannual study that looks at women entrepre-neurs on a global basis. This research shows extremely positive trends of increasing numbers of women entrepreneurs around the globe. Some of these women are in extremely poor areas with very little economy, and with the support of funding structures like microfinance loans, they are able to create small businesses to support themselves and their families. Other research shows that when women have an income, they invest their money directly into their families, paying for things like better nutrition, health care, and education. But they also invest more into their communities, helping to create stronger economies and opportunity where little or none previously existed.[3]

Although entrepreneurship provides financial opportunity for women in a way that addresses the issue of gender bias in the job market, women involved in family businesses seem to be benefiting from a similar dynamic. Research shows that older generations in family businesses are increasingly open to the idea of the best person taking over, removing the gender bias that may previously have kept women out of family business leadership positions. There are, of course, still barriers to ascension, but the tide seems to be turning.[4]

But women business owners still face crucial barriers to success, like lower access to capital than their male counterparts.[5] What this means in everyday terms is that women business owners are having a harder time getting investment in their companies. Funding is crucial with new ventures as there is typically a period of time when the company or organization is not meeting its expenses with revenue, so the costs of everything from staff to office space to product development have to be met with cash that has not yet been earned.

The barriers women business owners face to funding feels strikingly similar to the issue of individual working women who face a financial barrier to success with the gender wage gap, earning on average 78 percent of what men earn for full-time work. Understanding finance and how investing works can help women break into some of these more male-centric areas of finance, which can help provide the crucial resource to get a new venture off the ground. This in turn provides opportunity for financial growth, flexibility, and self-actualization for women in all different fields.

The Value of Entrepreneurship Education

Because entrepreneurship is all about creativity and resourcefulness, tenacity and resiliency, there is huge value in teaching girls and women about entrepreneurship, even to those who might not want to own their own business one day. Learning how to embrace failure, and to use that failure as a foundation for a great success, a better idea, or a piece of the puzzle leading ultimately to a real solution, is as powerful a trait as any. Entrepreneurship allows incredible opportunity for self-development, strength- and confidence-building, and more avenues to success.

The financial side of entrepreneurship, in a financial education context, is equally important and valuable. Personal and business finance have areas of overlap, but for those who may not find learning personal finance to be particularly compelling, entrepreneurial finance can provide a more exciting and engaging context to learn about money.

In a similar vein, teens who work in their younger years earn more money when they are older and have an easier time finding a job, research shows. It makes a lot of sense when you think about it. The job search requires research, organization, positive self-presentation, and persistence. Actually holding and keeping the job can give teens experience with being on time, meeting deadlines, working with adults, and bearing responsibility. Earning a salary, as we have discussed in this book, is an excellent way to learn money management, especially when combined with budgeting and goal setting.

Let's break it down and look at the specifics to helping students set up new ventures, whether they are model companies or real ones. Here's how it works in my classes:

Students work in teams. Ideally students will work together and collaborate in teams but also specialize in certain areas just like a team would. Students can focus on their area of their greatest interest or skill, including management, product development, financial analysis, marketing and sales, and funding.

Start with an idea. Each team needs to come up with an idea. In fact, the teams can come together based on shared interest in an idea, or an area on which to focus. Where does the idea come from? It can be anything from doing something you love, to finding the solution to a problem that hasn't been solved yet, to finding a better way of doing things. The idea can be a service, or a product, or even a method. It can be a social project, meaning, providing a service or something similar to the needy where profit is not the motive. It can also be a product or service that will make a profit.

Company description, organization, and management. From the idea phase, the team can develop a general idea of how the company (for-profit), or organization (nonprofit), is going to look. This means setting up a structure and defining roles within the company. The roles would include job descriptions that outline what each team member is responsible for.

Define your product. Once the team has an idea, it needs to specifically define the product. This area can be called "Product Development," where the general idea that the team came up with is refined by an individual on the team or a smaller group. Product development is important not just because it defines the product, and by extension, the purpose of the company. But product development is also important to create a plan of how the product will additionally be created, including all of the development planning, timetable, and funding needed. The product development schedule will also help dictate the sales and marketing plan and schedule, as well as the need for any start-up funding.

Analyze the market and the competition. It is critical to analyze both the market for the product or service and the competition. Some people call this a SWOT analysis, looking at strengths, weaknesses, opportunities, and threats. When analyzing the market for the product or service, the following questions need to be asked:

- Who would buy it?
- Why?
- What would they pay for it?

When doing an analysis of the competition, the following questions need to be asked:

- Who else is doing it?
- How is their way different than yours?
- Why is your way better?

The valuable lesson and learning from the SWOT analysis is that it gives the team the opportunity to focus on the strengths and opportunities of the product and the company, which are probably very clear and most likely drove the original idea generation in the first place.

But the analysis of weaknesses and threats is every bit as critical for a couple of important reasons. First, the success of a product may very well have more to do than figuring out its weaknesses than its strengths. It is easy to focus on the positives, and much harder to have the self-awareness to see the weaknesses and threats. Dealing with the negative issues will have a lot to do with making the company a success. Additionally, if any funding is being sought, it is important to be sure investors and donors understand that the company is well aware of weaknesses and threats, and has a plan to deal with them. Otherwise, the team will not seem as likely to be able to achieve success.

Marketing and Sales

Marketing is in part about how the company or organization communicates about its product or service. Communicating about a new idea means figuring out who is going to buy it, and how much they are willing to pay for it, and how they are going to get it. That is where sales comes in.

Marketing can also be about positioning, which means expressing to the targeted consumer or user how the product or service and be used, why it is beneficial to them in general, and how specifically it will help or serve them in some way better than the competition. The market analysis you did earlier should inform this process. The market analysis also informs your sales efforts. Understanding who you are selling to, how much they are willing to pay, and what other companies or organizations charge for the business or service is critical for setting your own pricing, and ultimately, doing your financial analysis. Additionally, knowing the best sales channel can help bring success, whether it's online, in a retail store, or some other method of sales.

Financial Projections

Financial projections for the company are important, but definitely tricky, because with any new company or product, there are a lot of unknowns. Financial projections are needed for several reasons. First, every new business has start-up costs—to pay the team, office space, product development, and marketing and communications. Then there is the issue of when the company or organization will start bringing in revenue and when it will hit a "break-even" point, meaning when the expenses, or costs of the company, will be met squarely by the revenue, or the income that is brought in from the sale of the product or service.

In order to run the company and get things started, it is important to know how much of an initial investment is needed. It is also important as the company moves forward to know when the break-even point will be, because additional investment or donations will be needed up until that point.

Funding Options and Business Plan

In order to get a business started, start-up costs, as described in the previous section, need to be funded. This can be done through investors, or through the owners of the company putting in their own money, or through donations, in the case of a nonprofit company. In order to receive outside funding from investors or donors, the team will need to put together a business plan that outlines all of the areas just covered.

The goal of the business plan is to describe the plan for the company, with specific information about financial needs, which respond to a careful and thorough analysis of start-up costs. The business plan also has another very important purpose, which is to convince potential investors or donors that not only does the company have a good, financially viable idea for a product or a service, but also that the team can actually make it happen. It is a critical document and needs to be thorough but clear.

Social Entrepreneurship and Girls

Social entrepreneurship is a fantastic way to teach girls and young women about money, management, idea generation, and creativity. Social entrepreneurship is the way to solve the world's problems, by applying creativity, ingenuity, and maybe even a "business" model, to social problems governments have not been able to solve. Wendy Kopp, who founded Teach for America, and Muhammad Yunus, who founded Grameen Bank, are fantastic role models in terms of their effectiveness as entrepreneurs, but also their contributions to the world.

The beauty of social entrepreneurship is it can be a very engaging course as students attempt to solve the world's problems in innovative ways, with new approaches to the problems, and positive predicted outcomes. It fits the model of "doing well by doing good," so that individuals can have the experience of entrepreneurs including self-management, creativity, tenacity, and running their own business, but actually changing the world in the process.

Most entrepreneurship education involves experiential learning, which is a powerful way to engage students. Social entrepreneurship education is an effective way to teach girls about money, as well as other empowering areas. Social entrepreneurship education typically involves the following topics and learning outcomes:

- Goal setting
- Idea generation
- Opportunity recognition
- Mission identification
- Financial analysis
- Presentation skills

I did a very interesting program made up of high school girls from the United States and China, and with the help of some very talented women college students, I taught economics and financial understanding through social entrepreneurship. The students were divided into groups and developed model projects while also having classroom time learning entrepreneurship and finance.

The student groups were charged with coming up with organizations that solved social challenges. Over the course of several hours, the students had to come up with an idea, design an organization around it, and grapple with all of the issues of launching a new venture. The students had to develop the idea, come up with a management structure, have a marketing and communications plan, do the financial projections, and finally, put everything into a well-articulated presentation and present their organization before a panel of expert judges for feedback.

The social entrepreneurship projects that the students developed were extraordinary in their creativity and potential effectiveness. The students also worked with each other very effectively, even though many had not known each other before the program. That kind of teamwork is a critical skill for all students given the demands of the modern workplace.

The students did a brilliant job presenting their model organizations in front of a panel of experts we had assembled for the class. They put together presentations and did elevator pitches, just as they would have to if presenting to funders or donors. The students practiced their speaking with feedback from the college student TAs and prepared themselves as well as possible. After the presentations, each team fielded questions from the experts, having to handle certain analyses on the spot.

I have noticed in recent years more and more schools begin to take a look at introducing entrepreneurship, including social entrepreneurship, into their curricula. In particular, I have seen all-girls' schools begin to look into this possibility, which is an interesting trend and a sign of the potential effectiveness of this type of education for girls.

Social entrepreneurship also provides some pretty amazing role models for girls and young women. Social entrepreneurship is an opportunity for girls and young women to expand their minds and put their critical thinking skills and creativity to work to solve the world's problems. It is an engaging method to teach about finance and economics, and is an experiential approach that makes for particularly effective learning. Social entrepreneurship is also a way for a young woman to start her very own organization, which is a fun and meaningful extracurricular or summer activity that may eventually change the world.

Do Try This at Home!

One great exercise is for teens to find a job. But it is no secret that finding a job as a teenager can be pretty challenging for lots of reasons.

Here is an exercise to help girls find their way into the workforce:

* *Reflect.* Take some time to think about what you are interested in and how that might translate into a part-time job. Also think about what you are good at and where you have natural talent. You can try the "What Am I Good At"

exercise from Chapter 3. Write down a list of things you are interested in, and a list or your talents and skills, and see what overlaps.

- *Research.* Research the job market in your area. You should look at stores, restaurants, and community centers and learn who might be hiring and what types of skills they require. You can research online, and this type of research is helpful. But there is no substitute for pounding the pavement—a lot can be learned by visiting a store, talking to the salespeople, and watching the customer flow.

- *Prepare.* Having a resume at this age not only makes you look more professional, but putting together a resume is excellent practice for the future and gives a clear idea that a career is built through education and experience. Self-introduction and interview practice are also critical for most teens. I have found teenaged girls are not always comfortable talking about their strengths—this needs to be practiced.

- *Invent.* It may be that a preestablished job is not the right fit for you. Maybe you are more interested in working with children, animals, gardens, or creating your own wares to sell. Inventing a job, meaning, becoming an entrepreneur to develop a business in babysitting, tutoring, dog walking or cat feeding, plant watering or garden tending, or creating things to sell, is a slam dunk as it not only provides work experience and income, it also provides invaluable experience in entrepreneurship.

Discussion Points

Here are some additional discussion points you can share with the young woman in your life about entrepreneurship. Financial conversations using these discussion points can be had whenever is convenient—at breakfast, in the car, during family time, or a specially prescribed time to talk about money in a group or a club.

1. *Entrepreneurship is a creative process.* Entrepreneurship can be called "creative destruction," because it finds a new and better way to do something, which means it replaces a less effective way. As such, entrepreneurship is a very creative process, because you have to think of all different ideas and approaches to make something better, or invent something new all together.

2. *Entrepreneurship is a great way to learn about money.* When you have your own business, you have to manage the financial picture just like you would your own. So you have to budget and plan, and have expectations about how much money you are earning and how much money you are spending. You have to think about taxes and insurance to make sure you are prepared and protected. Investing comes into play when you think about purchases you have to make with your hard-earned

revenue, which will actually help the business produce more income, like a positive rate of return.

3. *Entrepreneurship role models.* Let's talk about some of the different entrepreneurs who you think are really impressive and who are role models for you.

4. *Different types of ventures.* New ventures can be for-profit, or commercial, meaning they exist to make a profit. They can also be nonprofit, or more socially minded. Usually, commercial ventures invent things for sale, like new products for different areas of life. Social ventures typically seek to solve a societal problem, like finding a way to bring water to a village in a poor country.

FIND A JOB!

1. Reflect on your skills, talents, and interests.
2. Research job possibilities in your area.
3. Prepare a resume and practice interviewing.
4. Start your own business!

CHAPTER TWELVE

From Here: How to Keep the Learning and Empowerment Going

We have talked a great deal in this book about women earning less, the metaphorical glass ceiling that prevents women from rising frequently to executive levels, the impossible work-life balance that working mothers face. Studies continue to bemoan women's lack of financial literacy. Women are poorer than men, on average, and almost twice as likely to end their lives below the poverty line.[1]

But what happens when women do have money?

Despite all the negative reports and statistics out there about women's wealth capability, women are at the same time viewed to be a growing economic force—an "emerging market," by some reports. Different studies show women controlling large amounts of wealth in the next couple of decades, either through earned, inherited, or marital income.[2]

Financial education is important, no matter the wealth level. And across income levels, women reflect similar sentiments around money. Studies show that women's financial goals tend to focus on family, education, health, and community.

Women also want—and need—financial flexibility, to deal with what may come up in their lives. Women tend to be the caregivers for their children and their parents. Divorce is also common in the United States, and the end of marriage can need financial flexibility as well.

When women engage with money, they engage around their priorities and goals in life, which may be different than their male counterparts. For that reason, they need financial advisers who can connect on those touch points, and create a program that provides understanding and confidence, as well as financial management, to meet their goals.

Anecdotal evidence and more formal research show that when women work with a financial adviser, they want more of a holistic experience. In my classes with high school girls, many of them want to go into the financial industry when they are done with school. These young women are interested in money and engaged with their financial learning. As I work with them, encouraging their interests and helping them learn, it is exciting to consider the possibility of a more inclusive financial services community that meets the needs of all people.

Signs are pointing to this evolution now, and as more and more girls and young women learn about money and gain economic possibility, they will be able to command the service that they need and deserve. How can we help them get there? One way is to bring theoretical financial learning more prominently into the practical world. What I have learned through working with girls and financial education for a number of years is that opportunities to demonstrate a growing mastery over money can be extremely engaging to girls and young women.

Looking back at the previous chapters in the book, we covered the following important financial management areas:

- Income: Learn Not to Underearn
- Budgeting and Saving: Needs versus Wants
- Simple and Compound Interest: You Can Understand This!
- Debt and Credit: Let's Manage This
- Investing and Mortgages: Girls Don't Need to Fall Behind
- Taxes Don't Have to Be a Dirty Word
- Insurance: The Ultimate Hedge
- Financial Information Sources: Education and Experts Matter
- Entrepreneurship: Think in a New Way

Although short exercises were provided to help integrate learning and understanding at the end of each chapter, we can take the learning a step further and combine some of the topics into activities that can provide benefits for a lifetime. Check them out!

Financial Nutrition® Activities

Open an IRA and Track Its Performance (Topics: Compounding and Investing)

What is an IRA? An IRA is short for an "individual retirement account." The goal of an IRA is to provide an investment vehicle to save and earn enough money to live on when you are retired and are no longer able to earn an income to support yourself. There are different kinds of IRAs, some that come through a job like a 401(k) or a 403(b), some that can be opened if you own your own business like a SEP IRA, and others that can be started by individuals, like a Roth IRA.

Although there are differences among these different investment vehicles, the goal is the same, to provide sufficient income for retirement. Starting an IRA early is a fantastic exercise for girls and young women, for many reasons. First, it is a great way to both learn about compounding and benefit from it. Compounding, as we discussed in Chapter 5, is an incredibly powerful force in finance. In brief, compounding is earning interest on interest (or paying interest on interest, as the case may be), as well as on principal. The more time your money has to be invested and compound returns, the greater advantage you have. In fact, as was discussed in Chapter 7, the earlier you start saving, the less you will actually have to put away to earn a large amount for retirement. And benefiting from compounding in this case means having financial security when you retire, without having to save every penny you earn to make that happen.

The other important area for women that opening an IRA addresses is investing. As we discussed in Chapter 7, women can be more risk-averse in their investing than men and do not always invest in assets that are as aggressive as they need to be to earn enough money for retirement. One way to learn about and get comfortable with investing is by doing it and experiencing the ups and downs of the market at a time when there is less at stake. One way to learn about the volatility of the market and how to benefit from it is by having an investment and monitoring it while reading about the markets.

So let's get started! Here are some steps to opening and monitoring an investment account, or IRA:

1. Research different mutual fund companies and decide which one you want to invest in. You can read about the companies on their websites.

2. Once you decide on a company, look at the different funds they offer. You may want to choose one that has a lot of diversification and low fees. One way to achieve both of those investment goals is to invest in an index

fund. The holdings in an index fund reflect those of a major financial index, like the S&P 500. The S&P 500 is an index that includes 500 large U.S. companies.

3. One way to choose an index fund is to compare its performance over 1, 5, and 10 years. The fund company's website will have information about each of the funds on their own page. Although performance is historical and does not predict the future, it is one of the measures investors use when determining how an investment might perform in the future.

4. You may also want to choose a fund with a low minimum investment. You can always add to it over time if you choose. If you are under 18 years old, you will need a parent or guardian help you sign up for the account.

5. Once you have purchased the mutual fund, you can start reading about the fund or the stocks in it. It is also a great idea to read about the stock market each day in a major newspaper or a major financial website.

Manage an Allowance or Earnings from an After-School Job (Topics: Income and Budgeting)

Earning an income is a wonderful way to learn about money and negotiating a salary, and also begin to learn about career ideas. The other opportunity when you earn money or receive an allowance is to set up a budget and follow it.

As we have discussed in Chapter 3, an income from a job is one of the primary ways to build wealth in the United States. It is important to know how to research income levels for different jobs and negotiate a competitive salary. Although income is one side of the wealth-building equation, the other side is spending. The more you spend, the less you can save and invest. So learning how to set up a budget to manage your spending is a great way to control your finances and learn to create financial stability.

Getting a job and managing your income is a great way to begin to learn the basics of building wealth. Finding a job you like is a lesson unto itself, but adding to that, finding a job that pays you what you are worth and negotiating the salary to achieve that, is a fantastic opportunity to lay the groundwork for real wealth-building at an age where you may not yet have to support yourself. It is an opportunity to experiment with different methods and figure out what you are good at.

Budgeting, as we discussed in Chapter 4, is the root of financial management and extremely empowering. Budgeting means having control of your money, which can be very emotional and difficult to manage. Budgeting means having a plan and being intentional with your spending, and very possibly having a goal for what you would like to spend the money on, or save it for. Pairing this focused, intentional goal setting and financial management with an income is a powerful force!

So let's get started!

1. First, ask yourself, what are you interested in? What do you like to do? What are you good at? After thinking about what you are interested in and what you are good at, then consider how that might translate into a part-time job. You can try the "What Am I Good At" exercise from Chapter 3. Write down a list of things you are interested in, and a list or your talents and skills, and see what overlaps.

2. Next, take some time to take a look at the part-time job market in your area, or the summer job market, depending on the time of year you are looking. Visit stores, restaurants, and community centers, and look online, to learn who might be hiring, and what types of skills they require. You might also think about doing work like babysitting, yard work, or dog or cat sitting.

3. One great way to look organized and professional to potential employers is to put together a resume. Creating a resume is excellent practice for the future and gives a clear idea that a career is built through education and experience.

4. The resume can be used is a basis for preparing for an interview. Women and girls can sometimes have a hard time talking about their value and strengths, so it is a really good idea to practice before an interview. It is also a way to learn how to explain your value to a potential employer. In preparation for the interview, you also should thoroughly research the job so that you understand it and can ask intelligent questions about it to demonstrate interest.

5. Ahead of the interview, it is also a good idea to research the salary for the position so you can negotiate the most competitive salary. You can research some types of jobs online, by region. You can also talk to people who are currently doing the job and see if they can share with you any information about the job.

6. Once you apply for and get the job, and negotiate a salary, you can set up a budget. As we discussed in Chapter 4, a budget is a spending plan, organized into categories. With a budget, you can decide how much you are going to spend each week or each month on different categories like food, entertainment, clothes, and saving.

7. The first piece of information you need is your income for that period of time. For example, if you want to make a monthly budget, you can use your expected monthly income to determine how much you have to allocate across the different categories.

8. Once you have created your budget, you can then follow the spending plan to keep your money organized, and potentially save.

Start Your Own Business (Topic: Entrepreneurship)

As you think about getting a job, or earning income and budgeting, or setting up an investment account, it may be that a preestablished job is not the right fit for you. You may want to be your own boss and have some great ideas you want to share with the world that might also earn you some income. Maybe you are disciplined, focused, creative, and hardworking, and want to try something on your own. If these things are true, entrepreneurship is for you!

Entrepreneurship is also a fantastic opportunity to start thinking creatively and being solution focused. Think about something that is needed in your community or an improvement on an existing product or service. Listen to the people around you and get a sense of what they are interested in and what is missing in their lives. Spend some time focusing on those less fortunate than you, and think of ways they could be helped more effectively than they might currently be. Pretty soon, you will have an assortment of ideas that just may translate into a new for-profit, or social venture.

The next steps then are tricky, as turning an idea into execution is not easy. But it is possible and also provides amazing experience with managing money.

So how do you get started?

1. First thing, think about whether you would like to start this business alone, or with a friend, or a group of friends. The upside of doing it yourself is complete control—you make all the decisions, you know what needs to get done, and you make sure it gets done. The downside, of course, is that you don't have anyone to lean on, share ideas with, or share the workload with. If you work with a friend or a team, you can collaborate and also specialize in areas you prefer or are better at. Each option has pros and cons; you just need to think about what is best for you.

2. Next, come up with an idea of what you want to do. You may already have one, which is why you wanted to start your own business in the first place. Maybe you want to do a job with an online focus, or work with people or children, or create something that you sell. You may provide a service, like babysitting, tutoring, dog walking or cat feeding, plant watering or garden tending.

   It helps if the idea is something you love to do and are good at, and provides something on the market that doesn't already exist, or provides a better way. The idea should be realistic, and for that reason, it does not hurt to start small. No matter what, you will get great experience with money and financial management, and you might even make some!

3. Next, think about how to bring this idea to fruition. What do you need to get there? This is another opportunity to revisit the idea of whether you start this company by yourself or with a friend or a group. In order to sell the product or the service you are developing, what needs to be in place in your company? If you do decide not to go it alone, it's a good idea to put together job descriptions of what each of the owners is responsible for.

4. Next, think about the product or service you are trying to develop and the market it fits in. Define your product, both by itself, and in comparison to its competition. For example, perhaps you would like to start an animal-sitting business. Look at what people are already doing in this space and how you can do it better and add value. Then, after analyzing the market and competition, define the service or product more specifically.

5. You are now going to need to get the word out about your business and also figure out how to sell your product or service. Will you advertise on the Internet, with flyers in local stores, by word of mouth? How much will your product or service cost? How can your market reach the product or service? These are all questions that need to be answered, and plans that need to be made.

6. Next, you need to do some financial projections for your business. First, figure out your start-up costs. These are the costs that it will take to get your business up and running before you are selling anything and bringing in revenue. Next, determine how much it will cost to run the business and when you think you will have enough revenue, or income, to meet those expenses. Finally, do an analysis of how long it will take and how much of your product it will take to earn a profit.

7. Finally, figure out if you can afford to fund the start-up costs on your own, or if you need a loan, or some form of investment. If you do borrow money from someone you know or in your family, remember to talk to them about whether or not you need to pay interest, and if so, how much. Then, factor in the interest costs to the financial projections you are doing for the company.

8. Once all of these things are sorted out, you can start your company. Good luck!

Financial Nutrition® Clubs

Financial Nutrition® is the name of this book and also the name of the method of financial learning we employ in the book. Financial Nutrition® is also a nonprofit organization focused on helping girls and women learn about money.

One way to keep the learning going is to form clubs at school, participate in conversations and debates, and work on projects together. Financial

Nutrition® also has a curriculum of six classes for financial education for girls, and networks are forming between schools that have the program. Networking is a great opportunity for girls and young women, and with the Financial Nutrition® Facebook page, networking is simple.

But let's break it down and take a look at why it's important for girls and young women to communicate with each other about money, and learn together.

1. It's easy to start a Financial Nutrition® club at your school. All you need is a group of girls who are interested in economic empowerment and learning more about how to manage their money to gain financial security and independence. The club can meet weekly or monthly to talk about current events around women and money, do activities like learning how to negotiate a salary, or do projects like investing or starting a company. We provide more information on how to set up a club in Appendix 1.

2. Financial Nutrition® also offers a curriculum that can be purchased or donated to your school. The curriculum has six classes that cover: The Context of Women and Money, Income and Salary Negotiations, Budgeting, Compound Interest, Debt and Credit Scores, and Banking Services. The program can be taught during the school day or as an after-school program. The curriculum comes all ready to teach, and we have more information about it in Appendix 2.

3. Networking is a great skill to know, and networking with other girls interested in economic empowerment and financial independence is even better! With the Financial Nutrition® Facebook page, girls from all over the country can network with each other and read posts that provide learning and ideas for economic empowerment for girls and women of all ages.

Conclusion

We have talked a lot in the book about the critical life issues surrounding girls and money confidence. Here on the threshold of adulthood, it is a great time to focus on how to solve those issues. Start thinking about what you can do now to help your daughter become a financially confident, successful, secure adult.

Here are a few ideas to get you started:

1. *Talk to your daughter about money.* Although money can be an uncomfortable topic, one good way to raise everyone's comfort level is to start talking about it.

2. *Encourage your daughter to learn about money.* Provide sources that teach about money and economics, from books specific to the topic, to a respectable daily news publication.

3. *Provide ways for your daughter to work with money.* Have your daughter track her spending, actively budget, and set goals for saving. Consider opening an investment account that you manage together.

4. *Educate yourself.* Not only will you know more and can then share what you learn, you will be modeling the behavior of life-long learning about money and finance.

5. *Find a program.* If financially educating your daughter feels overwhelming, or if you would like some support in the process, find a program that can educate your daughter and provide support for you too.

Financial education is not only the gift that keeps giving, it is one of the surest ways to start on the path to meeting financial goals and gaining a comfort and confidence with money. There is no reason we should not all have that gift.

Happy financial success and economic empowerment from Financial Nutrition®!

Appendix 1:
Financial Nutrition® Clubs

One great way to keep the learning and empowerment going is by starting a Financial Nutrition® club at your high school or college. The mission of Financial Nutrition® is financial education for girls' economic empowerment. One great way to become empowered is to empower yourself. Another great way is to build a community where everyone can help each other. Starting a club and building a strong, supportive community of young women is a surefire way to become independent and savvy.

To help you get started, here is a framework you can follow. Keep in mind, however, that it is always best to figure out what works well for your school, community, and what the members would like to focus on.

Financial Nutrition® Club Framework

1. *Choose a meeting time.* Think about once a week, or every two weeks, or even once a month if that is the only time that works. Find a day and time that fits most people's schedules. This may be after school, early evening, or even at night or on the weekend if everyone is really busy.

2. *Find a meeting location.* Your school may have spaces for clubs to meet, or you could even go to a restaurant or coffee place that provides room for groups to sit around and talk while enjoying a meal or a cup of coffee. It's good to pick a place that is consistent and reliable, so that the club has a firm foundation.

3. *Find some friends.* Talk to people you know who share an interest in financial empowerment. Talk to them about your idea and see if you can get a core group together to get a club started.

4. *Pick meeting topics.* There are a variety of themes you can pursue, but here are a few to try.

   Gender wage gap. Find articles to discuss about women's salary discrepancies. Look at the latest trends and research. Answer questions like, how does discrimination play a role? Do women need to be more activist in salary negotiations? What kinds of choices would you make in that situation? Are there longer-term solutions?

   Value and worth. Talk to each other about what you like about yourself and what you are good at. Have discussions about how these natural talents and areas of interest can be manifested in careers in the future. Brainstorm different kinds of jobs, or areas, each member is interested in going into.

   Money management. Discuss different ways members manage their money, including goal setting, budgeting, and saving. Share your successes and effective practices, and also areas where you would like to improve. Help each other set goals for improvement, and then follow up and support each other in future meetings.

   Investing. Read about and discuss the financial markets and economy. Talk about what kinds of investments might do well in the current economy and the types of investing you are interested in. Share experiences each member has or hopes to have in the future with investing.

   Role models. Talk about women role models that members aspire to be like. These could be business owners, artists, executives, mothers, elected officials, or anybody who is successful and happy in what she is doing.

5. *Pick group projects.* It might be a great experience for the clubs, in additional meetings and discussions, to do some experiential learning together with projects. There are a variety of projects you can pursue, but here are a few to try:

   Start a business. This could be a real business or social venture, or a model one. You can follow the instructions above in the chapter and work together as a group to get the company going, with each member taking a different role.

   Build a portfolio. Put those market and investing discussions into action! Build a model portfolio, discussing what kinds of investments to buy and why. Put everything in a spreadsheet, and track it over time to see how it performs.

   Find a job. One interesting project is for members to support and counsel each other as you look for jobs. You can do a resume-writing workshop where members get their resumes together and also practice job interviews. Members can share with the group their experiences with the process and get productive support and feedback.

Field trips. Some interesting field trips might involve visits to women-owned companies, talks on money management and investing, and trips to meet with other Financial Nutrition® clubs in your area.

6. *Market and communicate.* Once the club has core membership, a meeting time and location, and some topics and projects, it's time to spread the word! Figure out if how it works best to communicate at your school—social media, flyers in the hallway, email, word of mouth. Send out information about the club before every meeting, and try to be as clear as possible about the goals of the club.

7. *Share the news.* When things are up and running, share your fun, events, learning, and empowerment on the Financial Nutrition® Facebook page. It's a great opportunity to share ideas, and successes, and learning experiences. We cannot wait to hear from you!

Appendix 2: Financial Nutrition® Curriculum

The Financial Nutrition® curriculum is a six-course curriculum designed to advance the learning and disposition of girls and women in the areas of money management and financial literacy. The curriculum includes a Teacher's Guide with step-by-step instructions for each class, PowerPoint presentations with discussion points, activities with instructions, and student worksheets. The curriculum is grounded in research and piloted successfully with proven knowledge mastery and engagement.

Class 1: Context of Women and Money

The Context of Women and Money class introduces the unique issues that women face with financial management and also sets the stage for the following classes. This class will provide a lot of information about women in the workforce, women's earnings, and other issues women face.

Class 2: Income and Salary Negotiations

The Income and Salary Negotiations class will focus on the gender wage gap, including the information that the gap begins at college graduation. The presentation for this class is shorter, so that time can be spent on the salary-negotiation activity. This activity is meant to give the students both the experience of negotiating for a job and the experience of saying "No" to the offer made. Studies have shown that college women graduates do not negotiate their starting salary, which can cost them upwards of half a million dollars over a lifetime.

Class 3: Budgeting

The Budgeting class focuses on the foundational understanding of "needs" and "wants," as well as goal setting, to build a knowledge of planning for spending and saving. The class provides an explanation of a "budget" as a tool for managing monthly income. The budgeting activity provides an opportunity for the students to have hands-on experience with creating a budget for their lives as adults and comparing how different levels of spending impact debt and savings.

Class 4: Simple and Compound Interest

The Simple and Compound Interest class focuses on an understanding of interest as the cost of money. Interest applies both when money is borrowed or when it is saved and invested. Simple interest is interest on principal, which is the amount of money originally borrowed. Compound interest is a more complex formula, as it involves both interest on principal and interest on interest. Compound interest also accumulates much more quickly than simple interest. This can work positively when interest is being compounded over time on savings or an investment. It can be a financial detriment when interest is compounding on debt, as it grows more quickly, and more is owed.

Class 5: Debt and Credit Scores

The Debt and Credit Scores class focuses on how debt works and how lenders evaluate borrowers. The presentation shows the elements of a loan, including principal, interest, and term, and discusses the idea of creditworthiness, meaning the likelihood a borrower will repay a loan in full and on time. The class also focuses on credit scores and what kind of information goes into them. The activity will involve going into greater detail in learning what information goes into a credit score, and what information does not, so that students can have a basic understanding of how to build strong credit.

Class 6: Banking Services

The Banking Services class focuses on the services that banks and other financial institutions provide consumers, checking and savings accounts, and ATM cards. Finding low-cost, high-quality services is emphasized. There is also some discussion about online banking services and the importance of security in that area. The lesson ends with a broader discussion of credit cards, and the activity is focused on learning to read a credit card statement.

Notes

Preface

1. Donohue, Melissa. "Financial Literacy and Women: Overcoming the Barriers." Scholarworks @UMass Amherst. May 13, 2011. Accessed March 2, 2017.

2. Ibid.

3. Ibid.

4. United States Department of Labor. "Women in the Labor Force in 2010." Accessed March 2, 2017. https://www.dol.gov/wb/factsheets/Qf-laborforce-10.htm.

5. "Chapter 3: Obstacles to Female Leadership." Pew Research Center's Social & Demographic Trends Project. January 14, 2015. Accessed March 13, 2017. http://www.pewsocialtrends.org/2015/01/14/chapter-3-obstacles-to-female -leadership.

6. Hicken, Melanie. "Why Many Retired Women Live in Poverty." *CNNMoney*. May 13, 2014. Accessed March 2, 2017. http://money.cnn.com/2014/05/13 /retirement/retirement-women/index.html.

7. Donohue, Melissa. "Financial Literacy and Women: Overcoming the Barriers." Scholarworks @UMass Amherst. May 13, 2011. Accessed March 2, 2017.

8. "Science & Engineering Degree Attainment: 2004–2014." National Student Clearinghouse Research Center. January 5, 2016. Accessed March 13, 2017. http://nscresearchcenter.org/snapshotreport-degreeattainment15.

9. "T. Rowe Price 6th Annual Parents, Kids & Money Survey." T. Rowe Price. August 2014. Accessed March 2, 2017. https://www.slideshare.net/TRowePrice /2014-parents-kids-money-survey-supplemental-data.

10. Donohue, Melissa. "Financial Literacy and Women: Overcoming the Barriers." Scholarworks @UMass Amherst. May 13, 2011. Accessed March 2, 2017.

11. Ibid.

Chapter 1

1. United States Department of Labor. "Women's Bureau: Data & Statistics." Accessed March 2, 2017. https://www.dol.gov/wb/stats/stats_data.htm.

2. Ibid.

3. Wang, Wendy, Kim Parker, and Paul Taylor. "Breadwinner Moms." Pew Research Center's Social & Demographic Trends Project. May 28, 2013. Accessed March 2, 2017. http://www.pewsocialtrends.org/2013/05/29/breadwinner-moms.

4. Donohue, Melissa. "Financial Literacy and Women: Overcoming the Barriers." Scholarworks @UMass Amherst. May 13, 2011. Accessed March 2, 2017.

5. Hicken, Melanie. "Why Many Retired Women Live in Poverty." *CNNMoney*. May 13, 2014. Accessed March 2, 2017. http://money.cnn.com/2014/05/13/retirement/retirement-women/index.html.

6. Gilligan, Carol. *In a Different Voice: Psychological Theory and Women's Development*. Cambridge, MA: Harvard University Press, 2016.

7. Donohue, Melissa. "Financial Literacy and Women: Overcoming the Barriers." Scholarworks @UMass Amherst. May 13, 2011. Accessed March 2, 2017.

8. "The Persistence of Male Power and Prestige in the Professions: Report on the Professions of Law, Medicine, and Science & Engineering." Center for Research on Gender in the Professions. March 2013. Accessed March 13, 2017. http://crg-stemm.ucsd.edu/_files/articles/PersistenceofMalePowerandPrestigeintheProfessionsReportwithCaseStudies.pdf.

9. Weber, Lauren. "And the Highest-Paid College Majors Are. . . ." *The Wall Street Journal*. May 16, 2013. Accessed March 2, 2017. http://blogs.wsj.com/atwork/2013/04/29/and-the-highest-paid-college-majors-are.

10. United States Department of Labor. "Women's Bureau: Data & Statistics." Accessed March 2, 2017. https://www.dol.gov/wb/stats/stats_data.htm.

Chapter 2

1. Hicken, Melanie. "Why Many Retired Women Live in Poverty." *CNNMoney*. May 13, 2014. Accessed March 2, 2017. http://money.cnn.com/2014/05/13/retirement/retirement-women/index.html.

2. Galbraith, Sasha. "Financial Services: The Industry Women Love to Hate." *Forbes*. January 2, 2012. Accessed March 13, 2017. https://www.forbes.com/sites/sashagalbraith/2011/03/18/financial-services-the-industry-women-love-to-hate/#58d5861978a7.

3. Ryan, Wendy, and Aaron Gouveia. "Why Women Don't Negotiate." Salary.com. Accessed March 13, 2017. http://www.salary.com/why-women-don-t-negotiate.

4. Goudreau, Jenna. "Failing to Negotiate Your First Salary Could Cost You Half a Million Dollars." *Business Insider.* June 23, 2014. Accessed March 13, 2017. http://www.businessinsider.com/millennials-and-negotiating-salaries-2014-6.

Chapter 3

1. Goudreau, Jenna. "Failing to Negotiate Your First Salary Could Cost You Half a Million Dollars." *Business Insider.* June 23, 2014. Accessed March 13, 2017. http://www.businessinsider.com/millennials-and-negotiating-salaries-2014-6.

2. Fairbanks, Amanda M. "'They Don't Negotiate': Why Young Women College Graduates Are Still Paid Less Than Men." *The Huffington Post.* June 13, 2011. Accessed March 3, 2017. http://www.huffingtonpost.com/2011/06/13/negotiate -young-women-college-graduates-first-job_n_875650.html.

3. United States Department of Labor. "Women's Bureau: Data & Statistics." Accessed March 2, 2017. https://www.dol.gov/wb/stats/stats_data.htm.

4. Lam, Bourree. "Why Does Progress on Women's Wages Seem to Be Stalling?" *The Atlantic.* November 17, 2015. Accessed March 13, 2017. https://www.the atlantic.com/business/archive/2015/11/gender-gap-women-wages-2015/415884.

5. Budig, Michelle J. "The Fatherhood Bonus and the Motherhood Penalty: Parenthood and the Gender Gap in Pay." *Third Way.* Accessed March 13, 2017. http://www.thirdway.org/report/the-fatherhood-bonus-and-the-motherhood -penalty-parenthood-and-the-gender-gap-in-pay.

6. "Pay Equity Information." Accessed March 13, 2017. https://www.pay -equity.org/info-time.html.

7. Bolotnikova, Marina N. "Reassessing the Gender Wage Gap." *Harvard Magazine.* April 15, 2016. Accessed March 13, 2017. http://harvardmagazine.com /2016/05/reassessing-the-gender-wage-gap.

8. Goetz, Lisa. "Top 10 Most Expensive Cities in the U.S." *Investopedia.* August 9, 2016. Accessed March 13, 2017. http://www.investopedia.com/articles /personal-finance/080916/top-10-most-expensive-cities-us.asp.

9. Kane, Libby. "Student Loan Debt in the US Has Topped $1.3 Trillion." *Business Insider.* January 12, 2016. Accessed March 13, 2017. http://www .businessinsider.com/student-loan-debt-state-of-the-union-2016-1.

10. Zumbrun, Josh. "Younger Generation Faces a Savings Deficit." *The Wall Street Journal.* November 9, 2014. Accessed March 13, 2017. https://www.wsj.com /articles/savings-turn-negative-for-younger-generation-1415572405.

11. Ellis, Blake. "Millennials 'Overwhelmed' by Debt." *CNNMoney.* Accessed March 13, 2017. http://money.cnn.com/2014/06/11/pf/millennials-debt.

12. Heimlich, Russell. "Young Women Surpass Young Men in Career Aspirations." Pew Research Center. May 2, 2012. Accessed March 13, 2017. http://www .pewresearch.org/fact-tank/2012/05/03/young-women-surpass-young-men-in -career-aspirations.

13. Lopez, Mark Hugo, and Ana Gonzalez-Barrera. "Women's College Enrollment Gains Leave Men Behind." Pew Research Center. March 6, 2014. Accessed March 13, 2017. http://www.pewresearch.org/fact-tank/2014/03/06/womens -college-enrollment-gains-leave-men-behind.

14. Sandberg, Sheryl. *Lean in: Women, Work, and the Will to Lead.* New York: Alfred A. Knopf, 2016.

15. Patten, Eileen, and Kim Parker. "A Gender Reversal on Career Aspirations." Pew Research Center's Social & Demographic Trends Project. April 19, 2012. Accessed March 13, 2017. http://www.pewsocialtrends.org/2012/04/19/a-gender -reversal-on-career-aspirations.

16. Folbre, Nancy. *The Invisible Heart: Economics and Family Values.* New York: The New Press, 2001.

17. Ibid.

18. Ibid.

19. "The Persistence of Male Power and Prestige in the Professions: Report on the Professions of Law, Medicine, and Science & Engineering." Center for Research on Gender in the Professions. March 2013. Accessed March 13, 2017. http://crg -stemm.ucsd.edu/_files/articles/PersistenceofMalePowerandPrestigeintheProfess ionsReportwithCaseStudies.pdf.

20. Weber, Lauren. "And the Highest-Paid College Majors Are. . . ." *The Wall Street Journal*. May 16, 2013. Accessed March 2, 2017. http://blogs.wsj.com/atwork /2013/04/29/and-the-highest-paid-college-majors-are.

21. Zeldin, Amy L., and Frank Pajares. "Against the Odds: Self-Efficacy Beliefs of Women in Mathematical, Scientific, and Technological Careers." *American Educational Research Journal* 37, no. 1 (2000): 215–46. http://www.jstor.org/stable/1163477.

22. Dweck, Carol S. "Is Math a Gift? Beliefs That Put Females at Risk." Accessed March 2, 2017. https://psychology.stanford.edu/sites/all/files/cdweckmathgift_0 .pdf.

23. Carnevale, Anthony P., Stephen J. Rose, and Ban Cheah. "The College Payoff: Education, Occupations, Lifetime Earnings." The Georgetown University Center on Education and the Workforce. Accessed March 13, 2017. https://cew .georgetown.edu/wp-content/uploads/2014/11/collegepayoff-complete.pdf.

Chapter 4

1. Hicken, Melanie. "Why Many Retired Women Live in Poverty." *CNNMoney*. May 13, 2014. Accessed March 2, 2017.

2. Ibid.

3. United States Department of Labor. "Women's Bureau: Data & Statistics." Accessed March 2, 2017. https://www.dol.gov/wb/stats/stats_data.htm.

4. "Vanguard Examines 401(k) Behavior/Outcome Gender Paradox." Pressroom. Accessed March 13, 2017. https://pressroom.vanguard.com/news/Press _Release_Women_and_DC_plans_CRR_paper_110315.html.

5. United States Department of Labor. "Women's Bureau: Data & Statistics." Accessed March 2, 2017. https://www.dol.gov/wb/stats/stats_data.htm.

6. Waid, Mikki. "An Uphill Climb: Women Face Greater Obstacles to Retirement Security." AARP. April 2013. Accessed March 13, 2017.

7. "Calculators: Life Expectancy." Accessed March 13, 2017. https://www.ssa .gov/planners/lifeexpectancy.html.

Chapter 5

1. "Commodity." Dictionary.com. Accessed March 13, 2017. http://www .dictionary.com/browse/commodity?s=t.

2. Goodreads. Accessed March 13, 2017. http://www.goodreads.com/quotes /76863-compound-interest-is-the-eighth-wonder-of-the-world-he.

3. "First OECD PISA Financial Literacy Test Finds Many Young People Confused by Money Matters." Accessed March 13, 2017. http://www.oecd.org /education/first-oecd-pisa-financial-literacy-test-finds-many-young-people -confused-by-money-matters.htm.

4. Beede, David, Tiffany Julian, David Langdon, George McKittrick, Beethika Khan, and Mark Doms. "Women in STEM: A Gender Gap to Innovation." U.S. Department of Commerce. August 2011. Accessed March 13, 2017. http://www .esa.doc.gov/sites/default/files/womeninstemagaptoinnovation8311.pdf.

5. "First OECD PISA Financial Literacy Test Finds Many Young People Confused by Money Matters." Accessed March 13, 2017. http://www.oecd.org/edu cation/first-oecd-pisa-financial-literacy-test-finds-many-young-people-confused -by-money-matters.htm.

6. Dweck, Carol S. "Is Math a Gift? Beliefs That Put Females at Risk." Accessed March 2, 2017. https://psychology.stanford.edu/sites/all/files/cdweckmathgift_0.pdf.

7. Lusardi, Annamaria, and Olivia S. Mitchell. "How Ordinary Consumers Make Complex Economic Decisions." March 2010. Accessed March 13, 2017. http://www.finrafoundation.org/web/groups/foundation/@foundation/docu ments/foundation/p122327.pdf.

Chapter 6

1. Donohue, Melissa. "Financial Literacy and Women: Overcoming the Barriers." Scholarworks @UMass Amherst. May 13, 2011. Accessed March 2, 2017.

2. "How FICO Credit Score Is Calculated." MyFICO. Accessed March 13, 2017. http://www.myfico.com/credit-education/whats-in-your-credit-score.

Chapter 7

1. Donohue, Melissa. "Financial Literacy and Women: Overcoming the Barriers." Scholarworks @UMass Amherst. May 13, 2011. Accessed March 2, 2017.

2. Ibid.

3. Carden, Robert. "Behavioral Economics Show That Women Tend to Make Better Investments than Men." *The Washington Post*. October 11, 2013. Accessed March 2, 2017. https://www.washingtonpost.com/business/behavioral-economics -show-that-women-tend-to-make-better-investments-than-men/2013/10/10 /5347f40e-2d50-11e3-97a3-ff2758228523_story.html.

4. "Women: Investing with a Purpose." Pershing. https://information.pershing .com/rs/651-GHF-471/images/per-premium-tl-women-investing-with-a -purpose.pdf.

5. Ibid.

6. Galbraith, Sasha. "Financial Services: The Industry Women Love to Hate." *Forbes*. January 2, 2012. Accessed March 13, 2017. https://www.forbes.com/sites /sashagalbraith/2011/03/18/financial-services-the-industry-women-love-to-hate /#58d5861978a7.

Chapter 8

1. Bullock, Christopher. *The Cobbler of Preston*. London: Publisher not identified, 1716.
2. United States Department of Labor. "Women's Bureau: Data & Statistics." Accessed March 2, 2017. https://www.dol.gov/wb/stats/stats_data.htm.
3. "Women in the Labor Force: A Databook." BLS Reports. December 2015. Accessed March 13, 2017. https://www.bls.gov/opub/reports/womens-databook /archive/women-in-the-labor-force-a-databook-2015.pdf.
4. "The 2016 State of Women-Owned Businesses Report." 2016. Accessed March 13, 2017. http://www.womenable.com/content/userfiles/2016_State_of _Women-Owned_Businesses_Executive_Report.pdf.

Chapter 9

1. Donohue, Melissa. "Financial Literacy and Women: Overcoming the Barriers." Scholarworks @UMass Amherst. May 13, 2011. Accessed March 2, 2017.
2. Ibid.
3. Ibid.
4. Hicken, Melanie. "Why Many Retired Women Live in Poverty." *CNNMoney*. May 13, 2014. Accessed March 2, 2017. http://money.cnn.com/2014/05/13 /retirement/retirement-women/index.html.
5. Wang, Wendy, Kim Parker, and Paul Taylor. "Breadwinner Moms." Pew Research Center's Social & Demographic Trends Project. May 28, 2013. Accessed March 2, 2017. http://www.pewsocialtrends.org/2013/05/29/breadwinner-moms.

Chapter 10

1. De Bassa Scheresberg, Carlo, Annamaria Lusardi, and Paul J. Yakoboski. "Working Women's Financial Capability: An Analysis across Family Status and Career Stages." TIAA-Cref Institute. May 2014. Accessed March 13, 2017. http:// media.wix.com/ugd/a738b9_95901ec612f44c92a789dd053ddd81ab.pdf.
2. "Women: Investing with a Purpose." Pershing. https://information.pershing .com/rs/651-GHF-471/images/per-premium-tl-women-investing-with-a-pur pose.pdf.

Chapter 11

1. Greene, Francis J., Liang Han, and Susan Marlow. "Like Mother, Like Daughter? Analyzing Maternal Influences upon Women's Entrepreneurial Propensity." *Entrepreneurship Theory and Practice* 37, no. 4 (2011): 687–711. doi:10.1111/ j.1540-6520.2011.00484.x.
2. "Number of Minority- and Women-Owned Firms on the Rise." The United States Census Bureau. December 15, 2015. Accessed March 13, 2017. https://www .census.gov/newsroom/press-releases/2015/cb15-209.html.

3. "How Women Entrepreneurs Are Transforming Economies and Communities." Babson College Blogs. Accessed March 13, 2017. http://blogs.babson.edu/leadership/2013/02/22/how-women-entrepreneurs-are-transforming-economies-and-communities.

4. Pinsker, Beth. "The 'and Daughter' Evolution of Family Businesses." Reuters. July 15, 2015. Accessed March 13, 2017. http://www.reuters.com/article/us-money-women-familybusiness-idUSKCN0PP1PU20150715.

5. Hecht, Jared. "Why Women Entrepreneurs Have a Harder Time Finding Funding." *Entrepreneur.* September 28, 2016. Accessed March 13, 2017. https://www.entrepreneur.com/article/281733.

Chapter 12

1. Hicken, Melanie. "Why Many Retired Women Live in Poverty." *CNNMoney.* May 13, 2014. Accessed March 2, 2017.

2. Galbraith, Sasha. "Financial Services: The Industry Women Love to Hate." *Forbes.* January 2, 2012. Accessed March 13, 2017. https://www.forbes.com/sites/sashagalbraith/2011/03/18/financial-services-the-industry-women-love-to-hate/#58d5861978a7.

Index

About the Author

Melissa Donohue, EdD, is president and founder of Financial Nutrition®, a nonprofit organization focused on girls' financial literacy and economic empowerment, and has more than 20 years of experience in finance, financial journalism, and financial education. She is a financial literacy expert with a research focus on women and adolescent girls, and she has extensive experience creating innovative and creative financial education curricula as well as direct classroom experience teaching teens about finance. Prior to her work in financial education, Donohue worked in financial journalism for nine years as a writer, editor, and segment producer, most recently at Bloomberg LP in New York. She also has significant experience in finance, having worked in emerging market debt trading and analysis at Swiss Bank Corporation and Wasserstein Perella, both in New York, and in alternative investment analysis in Amherst, Massachusetts. Donohue earned a doctorate in education from the University of Massachusetts, Amherst, where her dissertation research was focused on women's financial literacy, primarily on discovering the areas where women need financial education most. She also holds a master's degree in international affairs with a specialization in international banking and finance from Columbia University as well as a bachelor's degree in government from Oberlin College.